SURVIVING A TAKEOVER:
THE HUMAN FACTOR

Thank you for your interest
Hope you Enjoy The
book

SURVIVING A TAKEOVER:
THE HUMAN FACTOR

*Tips to Effectively Navigate Corporate
and Management Change*

Richard E. Whitman

SURVIVING A TAKEOVER: THE HUMAN FACTOR
TIPS TO EFFECTIVELY NAVIGATE CORPORATE AND MANAGEMENT CHANGE

iUniverse books may be ordered through booksellers or by contacting:

iUniverse
1663 Liberty Drive
Bloomington, IN 47403
www.iuniverse.com
1-800-Authors (1-800-288-4677)

Because of the dynamic nature of the Internet, any web addresses or links contained in this book may have changed since publication and may no longer be valid. The views expressed in this work are solely those of the author and do not necessarily reflect the views of the publisher, and the publisher hereby disclaims any responsibility for them.

Any people depicted in stock imagery provided by Getty Images are models, and such images are being used for illustrative purposes only.
Certain stock imagery © Getty Images.

ISBN: 978-1-5320-6704-4 (sc)
ISBN: 978-1-5320-6703-7 (e)

Library of Congress Control Number: 2019900904

Print information available on the last page.

iUniverse rev. date: 03/07/2019

DEDICATION

There are a number of people who helped me throughout my career. I was fortunate to have the support of my wife, Judy, who worked very hard to support the family while I traveled extensively and pursued my career. Our daughter Jennifer Paulett helped me prepare the book and my friend Neil Ferris contributed the chapters regarding the CEO, Errol Weiss was a co-worker, a customer, and a life- long mentor and friend. I was also pleased to have multiple mentors throughout my career beginning with Owen Brown and Murray Cook, RoseAnn Giordano and Harvey Weiss at DEC and for my first jobs out of DEC. Dan Woolley would become a mentor responsible for several jobs. Jason Mical and Yiannis Vassiliades were teammates at Silent Runner. My team at Global Integrity and Cyveillance included Jim Swinney, Jim Martin, Thomas Johnson, Don Sortor and Eric Baum. Panos Anastassiadis was a great mentor who continued support past our time at Cyveillance. And finally Doug Dangremond and Chris Coleman at LookingGlass helped me to realize that retirement is still possible. To all, I say Thank you for your help and support.

CONTENTS

Preface ix

Chapter 1   What Makes a Takeover Successful? 1
Chapter 2   So You Just Got Acquired 5
Chapter 3   The First Lesson in Management Change..................... 9
Chapter 4   Managing with Leadership and Motivation 12
Chapter 5   The Role of a Mentor in a Takeover or
            Management Change... 16
Chapter 6   My Fall from Grace 21
Chapter 7   Before the Takeover, New Management Teams
            Are Brought in for Survival................................ 25
Chapter 8   My First Small Company and a Near Takeover 28
Chapter 9   The Importance of Networking During Periods
            of Change 32
Chapter 10 How to Select a Potential Takeover Company............... 36
Chapter 11 My First Takeover 39
Chapter 12 A New Company and a Family Move 45
Chapter 13 Another Turn-Around and the First Sale.................... 52
Chapter 14 After the Takeover 55
Chapter 15 The New Requiem 58
Chapter 16 Strategies for Moving On..................................... 61
Chapter 17 My Option: The Path Least Traveled........................ 65
Chapter 18 The Master Plan 68
Chapter 19 The View from the Top 72
Chapter 20 The CEO of the Acquiring Company Evaluates
            the New Company.. 76

Chapter 21 The View from the CEO of the Acquired Company....... 79
Chapter 22 Selling the Company Again a Second Time.................... 82
Chapter 23 My Final Takeover... 85
Chapter 24 Decisions and Actions with Possible Negative
            Consequences 90
Chapter 25 Review of the Key Tips... 95

PREFACE

Have you ever been in a situation where you hear the words, "Our company has just been acquired?" Even if you expected it to happen, your first reaction is one of fear. What does this mean for me? Will I still have a job? Who will I work for? Does this mean I have to move? Will my project survive? What should I do? Even if you are one of those at the top, who have plenty of stock and will do well financially with the deal (which does not pertain to most of us), those questions still are top of mind. For most of us, the word *takeover* means change, and we don't typically like change. This book gives some guidance on what to expect and how to act when your firm is involved in a takeover. It is primarily written from the point of view of working for the company being taken over, although the acquirer can take away some valuable lessons as well.

This book looks at the experience of a number of takeovers, and even more management changes, and tells the story of what happens—and why—after a takeover is announced. It also tries to give some very practical tips as to what to look for, some strategies to employ, and just as important, what to avoid, and how not to act after you have been told that you will be acquired by a different company.

In many ways, a management change is just like a takeover but without the financial windfall. A new management team comes in and everything changes. When a management change occurs, all the dynamics in the firm change in the same manner as if there is a new company involved. It can really happen at any level and in any company. I treat a management change just like a takeover, and describe what you should do or avoid after a change.

I describe each of the takeovers or management changes that I was part of and give some direct hints as to how to act, what to do or avoid, and then tell the story behind why they worked or didn't work. In that way, you can put yourself in the situation and see the effect. In doing research on acquisitions, most advice I found seemed clinical and did not leave me with a path of what I should or should not do when faced with a takeover. This book attempts to bring the practical realities to life.

I have been in high-tech my entire career. I have worked for large companies, start-ups, turn-around companies, and for myself. I have been involved in eleven different takeovers and even more management changes. My score was that I was successful in navigating the change eight times, and three times it did not work out as well as I would have liked. I have been promoted and I have been fired. I certainly don't think that I know it all. However, I have been in many situations where I thought if only there was somebody that could give me advice as to what I could expect, it would have been helpful. I also have watched people make mistakes that cost them their positions. I came out of sales and marketing, and while I write from that perspective, I believe that the tips and experiences are relevant to all the other disciplines as well. I have managed technical experts, developers, product managers and consultants, and they are all looking for someone who can help them and has their back. An important point to remember is that because there have been so many takeovers in so many different industries, there are no absolutes. Every takeover is different, with little nuances. No matter what point I make, someone could give me an example of how it did or did not work in some particular merger. But most of the time, it will work the way I describe.

In order to survive a takeover, you must acknowledge and accept one guiding principle—***for a least the first six months, you are an idiot and they know everything.*** It has been true in every situation that I have been involved in or have heard about from others. If you can control your ego, accept the fact that while you used to be smart and now you know nothing, and you do not question the decisions they make, then you can actually win and improve your career. With the correct attitude and actions, you can improve your career faster than without a change. No matter the situation, it involves change, and change is difficult for everyone. The sole intent of the book is to provide some concrete suggestions to help you accept the change, or decide to put a strategy in place to move on.

CHAPTER 1

What Makes a Takeover Successful?

Investors are the ultimate judges of a successful takeover.

In the twenty-first century business world, mergers, acquisitions, and management changes happen in every industry and with great frequency. Many takeovers have worked and many more have been complete failures. Often you hear that culture makes or breaks a takeover. When cultures are totally different, they tend to compete when brought together. Take Daimler and Chrysler for example, where competing cultures certainly contributed to that failed union. Just imagine merging a company who makes the Dodge Dart with the company that produces the luxury Mercedes. When corporate cultures compete, it doesn't work at any level. That is generally because there almost is always a perceived winner (usually the company taking over) and a perceived loser, with key management positions being filled by the winner. In the Daimler example, another impediment to success was a language barrier, resulting in many meetings where both groups had to travel a great distance, as Daimler was headquartered in Germany, and Chrysler in Detroit, Michigan.

When Digital Equipment Corporation (DEC) was taken over by Compaq, there was a staid, old, consensus-management style company from New England being acquired by a fast-moving, top-down style company, with a brash, young management team from Texas who understood the PC market—a totally different market from Digital's. And surprise, surprise, it didn't work. When the new management team would fly in for meetings, they left feeling like they had communicated what they wanted and expected to be done. The Digital team felt like it was a suggestion and they needed several meetings to determine if they should do it, and then who was going to do the task at hand. The result was frustration on both sides. It wasn't until Compaq was taken over by HP that the Digital community began to feel like they had a chance to win. And it is not just in tech that these mergers have had difficult times integrating opposing cultures. In the financial services market, the takeover of Merrill Lynch by Bank of America was difficult, as was Washington Mutual's West Coast culture being integrated into the East Coast culture of JPMorgan Chase. In that case, the takeover was not easy for the community, management, or employees.

Before diving into how to behave and what to expect in a takeover, I want to look at why the takeover happens, and what ultimately determines its success. The number one reason an organization gets involved in a takeover is for investor return. Make no mistake; ***investors are the driving force behind any takeover.*** They put up the money for the company, they took the risk, and they ultimately make the decisions, and no decision is bigger than driving a takeover. It does not matter which side of the equation one is on, the board is involved in and drives the decisions in any takeover. ***The ultimate success criteria of any takeover is, "Did the investors get the return they wanted out of the deal?"***

There are a number of drivers that will motivate a board to explore or enter into an acquisition, and most are driven by growth. The best way for most companies to grow is through acquisitions. It is nearly impossible for large companies to grow large quickly without an acquisition. There are some notable exceptions—Google, Facebook and Tesla grew quickly without acquisitions, but as they grew larger, they too began to make acquisitions, sometimes for growth, but in most cases to gain new technology or markets. ***The best opportunity for a takeover is one that allows a company to enter and dominate a new market.*** That would be considered successful by any measure. The same goes for new product. Many of Computer Associates' best acquisitions over a twenty-year period were those that dominated a new product space, from Sort programs that enabled mainframe computers to operate more efficiently, to Identity and Access Management products where using a takeover allowed Computer Associates to become an industry leader in the security space.

One of the most successful and prevalent strategies for an acquisition has been companies attempting to enter or expand their government business. While the government does not do many direct acquisitions, they have a venture capital group called In-Q-Tel, whose goal is to fund start-ups so that they have access to the technology of small companies. More often than not, the government acquires a product or technology using a government contractor, or as they are often called, beltway bandits. There are many examples, as this has been done thousands of times with varying degrees of success. For each one that has succeeded, there have been failures. I worked for three different companies where government contractors were involved in acquisitions, each with a different level of success. The first one was the government contractor wanting to branch out into the commercial market, which is a common strategy for companies whose product was either paid for or sold into the government and then taken to the commercial market. While difficult, it can and does work. Fortunes have been made by companies whose products were initially funded by the government.

The other strategy is a company who is trying to get into the government market. I also have been involved in that kind of acquisition. The acquiring company is a contractor with a large government presence. They see a company with a product or technology that they believe can be sold into the government, if only that company had either the contracts—called contract vehicles—or the access to the right people. Remember, many times in the government marketplace, *who* you know is as important as *what* you know. While true in the commercial market, it is even more important in the government market. While this is a very good strategy and has been successful many times as well, one of the acquisitions I was involved with could not make it work.

So what happened in each of these cases? Each was different and there is no one reason for either success or failure. One contractor that I was involved with, QinetiQ North America, made seventeen acquisitions and was able to grow to a multi-billion dollar company in less than four years. They were successful early on for a number of reasons, including having a senior management team that came out of the government, with many high-level government connections. Later they struggled because they did a terrible job of integrating their various acquisitions into the company (a more detailed analysis is available in Chapter 11). In another case, a company owned by a government prime contractor, SAIC, was sold to a commercial company, Predictive Systems. While the company struggled later, they did an excellent job of integrating a computer security services company into their broad-based consulting company. And the third case involved a wholly-owned subsidiary of a prime contractor, Raytheon, being sold to a large software company. This acquisition went smoothly and the people and the product had a home for many years; although, it was never the financial success that was originally envisioned.

Another interesting strategy is for an acquisition to be made in order to take a competing product out of the market, and shut it down, with no interest in making it successful. Imagine this: you have a company that is a market leader and see a small company with a product that has the potential to become the market leader. What should you do? If you have big investments in capital and people in the product or service that has the dominant market share, by acquiring this new start-up, you can determine when or if that capability is introduced into the market. Using a non-compete with the management team just acquired, may buy the company two to three years to continue the market run. There are companies whose reputations are places where good products go to die, as was the case with Symantec and Computer Associates. However, the key driver for their acquisitions was the growth of the larger company and that made those transactions very successful.

While the success of an acquisition is judged based on the happiness of the investors, there are many other stakeholders on both sides of an acquisition. If your company was the one being taken over, who is affected by the takeover and what can they expect? I will delve extensively into those individuals and leave the board and the market to decide ultimate success.

CHAPTER 2

So You Just Got Acquired

As soon as the takeover is announced, it's all about me!

Everything is going so well. Your like your boss, you know what you are doing, you have the respect of your coworkers and you just received a big raise. Then you hear about or read the rumors: your company is about to be acquired. Your first thought is, "This could be good for me. These things happen all the time. What can I do to position myself?"

I want to start our journey at this point, because everything begins to change when the rumor of a takeover becomes real. We will start immediately before the takeover is public and continue throughout the period following the acquisition. Of course, every situation is a bit different, but there are many common mistakes to avoid and strategies to follow. My record is pretty good. Of the eleven takeovers that I was involved in, there were no homeruns. However, I would say the score is eight wins, two losses and one so-what.

A takeover is a bit like the American dream. It offers a chance for some people to partake in life-changing rewards. We strive for it. Join a small company, work very hard, the company does well, and a big company swoops in and buys it, and we all get rich. That's it, sign me up. And it happens this way with great frequency. Many of us know a friend or acquaintance that is now living on easy street because of a takeover or IPO. So why don't we all get excited when we hear the word acquisition?

Oh yes, there is another side of the equation. Who makes the money? Clearly the investors do well. Senior management usually does pretty well, either life-changing or enough to make a real difference. ***The question is, "How much stock do you own, and what does that mean for you?"*** If you are fortunate, you have some stock with some value and it is enough to make a difference. Those are the people we usually hear about, and with some companies, many employees have significant stock options, and it does make a real difference. HOWEVER, most of the time, those options do not go far down the corporate ladder, or you don't have enough to make a real difference. Now some of the other thoughts begin to come into play, namely, "What does this mean for me and my family?" You see, that is what it is all about. ***Our society teaches us to worry about, plan for, and take care of ME.***

Is the acquiring company headquartered nearby? Do they have their own infrastructure? Will this mean a move? Will my job be eliminated? What was the motive for the takeover, product, market penetration, or expansion? Should I start looking for another job? Do I want to be a part of a big company? How long do I have before the changes begin? Who will end up in the senior management positions? Will my boss stay? Will the kids have to change schools? Will my spouse have to change their job? These are all very real and difficult questions during this time of probable change.

There are generally two ways one hears about an acquisition. The first is by rumor. Many times the employees of a company have heard and know their company is "on the block." I always found this to be a difficult time, as it seems everything is frozen and people spend a lot of time around the water cooler speculating who, when and what, as the rumors swirl. It is terribly debilitating, as no one is concentrated on their real job, and in a sense, the company becomes paralyzed. New products slip, sales get postponed and it seems as if everything is on hold. Management has to be secretive during this period as the consequences are high if word gets out before the deal is completed. The deal could get queried, or people lose sight of their goals and the results are not as expected. But it is interesting that by watching who is downloading large amounts of data from the website, or by taking note of the unusually long offsite meetings, or who is visiting (like the management buy-out firms), you can easily figure out what is happening.

The other way people find out about a takeover is by complete surprise. An announcement is made usually to the press and analysts that Company A has just agreed to be acquired by or merged with Company B. The announcement is carefully prepared and has *all the correct spin to assure the employees of the acquiring company that this is a merger, not a takeover.* Horse manure! That is generally the work of the PR department attempting to assure people that they will all be well taken care of and everything will be okay. Ask the employees of Washington Mutual how they felt when they got the announcement of their acquisition by JPMorgan Chase. They were smart enough to know that most of their jobs would be eliminated or that they would have to move East—neither of which was very exciting.

After the announcement, generally there is a three to six month period where all of the legal work of the takeover is done, including the stock transfer, what is being procured, who will run the new company, and the marketing of the acquisition to the key stakeholders. All this has to be done with enough time to give proper notification to all those affected, especially the stockholders, which in many cases, have to vote on the acquisition. During this period, almost no productive work gets done. People become obsessed with the many things they don't know and can't control. You would think there would be a lot of jockeying for position, but in most cases, the amount of communication between the companies is limited in case the acquisition does not go through. *This is an excellent time for you to research the new company, their style, their management, their markets and the reasons for the acquisition*. By doing this research early, you are more prepared and knowledgeable than most of your colleagues when the integration meetings begin. Usually, there will be planning committees established to plan for life in the new company.

Finally, the big day arrives and the Human Relations department is King or Queen. This is their time of power and they are in charge. Meetings are set up to discuss the new company and how important the acquiring company is to the future. Generally, senior line managers are brought in to reassure the troops. Oftentimes you are given paperwork to sign, which will detail your position, your pay, your new team and manager, and any non-compete paperwork. This is a bit frustrating as you are being asked—no, actually demanded—to make decisions and to sign paperwork that is very important, and you don't have much information to make that decision. I recently heard of an acquisition that was announced on December 26, with stock options that had to be signed by December 28, and no one was around that was in a position to offer advice. Usually you are given two or three days to make a decision. Typically, you have little say and can make almost no changes to the new terms of your employment. This is important; particularly in the future if you decide to leave, because if early on you did not spend enough time or attention on this paperwork, it can now affect a move to another company. *My tip for this period is to review in detail the paperwork, do research into the new company, find out about the group you will be going into and their management, and try to influence your new position, title and income.* Understand that you will not have a great deal of influence, but the more you know and understand, the better it will be for you now and in the future.

Now the jockeying truly begins. From this day forward, your actions become important. *While you can't control everything, you can influence how you are viewed by the new management team.*

CHAPTER 3

The First Lesson in Management Change

The key is to quickly decide if you can adapt to this new style or want to leave.

In my first job after graduating from college, I learned a valuable lesson about management change: ***management change is never easy***; in fact, it is usually very difficult. I graduated from college in 1969 after spending five years of majoring in *having fun*. While it was a great time, it did little to prepare me for a job, let alone a career. When I graduated, I had no idea what I wanted to do. Shortly after one forgettable sales job, I took a job selling office equipment in the summer in Phoenix, Arizona, where my job was to check out three machines each day, and go door-to-door to businesses, and try to place them on trial. When the temperature is over 100 degrees, walking the streets is not much fun. However, by hard work or good fortune, or maybe a little of both, I did well and was soon promoted to selling computerized accounting machines.

My boss was named Bob McLuen—we called him the Silver Fox—a very smooth sales type who was a terrific motivator of his employees. He was the branch manager and hired a group who were all hard chargers, fun-loving, ex-jocks, who, when properly managed, could do anything. Bob was a true leader and taught most of us how to sell. Bob had many tricks and could reach just about everyone. We had many motivational meetings, and Bob would devise teams with the winners always getting a nice prize. He would involve spouses. He would work with his team to show them how to sell.

Everyone in the branch loved and responded well to Bob, and our office was consistently one of the leaders in the country. One of Bob's techniques was showcased best in the stockroom. The manager of the stockroom was an ornery, uneducated manager who drove everyone crazy, yet he would do anything for Bob. One day I asked Bob how he did this, and his answer was to treat everyone as if they were the vice president of their job, in this case the stockroom manager. When treated in that manner, people respond positively and will go the extra mile to please. I have adopted that technique and tried to make that my philosophy throughout the years, and it has served me well. I put many of Bob's management techniques into my bag of tricks.

Sure enough, just when everything was going well, we experienced our first management change. Bob was promoted to Chicago, and we got a new branch manager, a tightwad from Providence, Rhode Island, who had been in the clothing business and knew very little about selling computers and office equipment in the West. Everything changed!

It seemed like we quit learning and having fun. Sales staff began to leave, and the team was coming apart. For the first time in my short career, I could see that it was time to leave. I was just not willing to change what had been rewarding, educational, and fun to meet this new style. It was not that the new guy was bad, because in fact, he wasn't. However, he was not a leader. As I look back across my career, I have always been motivated by the carrot, not the stick. Certainly both forms of motivation work. Very successful companies like Oracle, Sun Microsystems, and DellEMC are examples of motivation by fear—produce or get out, with managers in all departments pushing their people hard to make their goals. From my first job under Bob McLuen, I learned that managing with positive reinforcement also could produce great results. ***Work hard, over-achieve your goals and have fun***. The result is great teamwork, where everyone contributes and the entire group does well.

What was interesting was that a management change had such a significant effect at all levels. When a new boss comes in, he or she will not do things the way the old boss did. They will quickly find or bring in people who will follow their lead. ***The key is to quickly decide if you can adapt to this new style, and if you can't, make plans to leave.*** Even if you work at a grocery store or a big box company, when the new boss comes in, at any level, decide quickly if you can work for this individual, learn and do well. If you can great, if you can't, get out.

CHAPTER 4

Managing with Leadership and Motivation

A motivated team will most often over-achieve their goals in any industry and at any level.

In 1974, I joined Digital Equipment Corporation, a fast growing mini-computer company headquartered in Maynard, Massachusetts. I was the company's first-ever sales trainee. I had sold accounting machines before, but these were real computers and I joined the division selling DECsystem-10s, a powerful mainframe that allowed many users to work simultaneously. The management team was very different from any I had ever experienced. Their philosophy was that selling large computers required more salesmanship and a sell-big, spend-big approach, because we were competing with IBM in the heart of their most successful market. We traveled extensively, entertained often, and never worried about expenses. I followed orders well and was selling large and spending large.

After several years on this team, sure enough, a management change occurred at the top of the Western Region, and a cheap, control-monger became the new Western Region manager. This is an example of where a management change at the top had a profound effect on 250-plus people spread over fifteen western states. Very soon, the rest of the previous management team departed the company. In one of his first moves, the new vice president sent out a notice to the entire region citing several examples of expense violations that would no longer be tolerated, and you guessed it, my name was on the list for flying first class on short trips and entertaining lavishly. I could have left like the others above me, or I could quickly change my ways and let everyone know it, especially the guy at the top. *A key in any management change is to realize that you may have to change your ways, but to be sure your management recognizes and acknowledges the change in your behavior.* New first and second line managers were brought in, and I soon became the model citizen, and the positive example of the new regime. I continued to sell well and, with my new behavior, I became one of the favorites in the entire region. In less than a year, I was promoted to first line manager, which necessitated a move to the San Francisco Bay region.

Managing a small team was a whole new experience. I followed a strategy of using leadership and motivation as my management style. I should add a word of caution on that style of management. You can easily be labeled a "players coach," or soft, or you want to be your employee's friend, or that you're just are not tough. *You must be tough and willing to do difficult jobs, but you can do them with class and respect, without resorting to yelling and threatening like some managers are known to do.*

It was during this time, I also realized that picking a mentor could help me move quickly up the ladder within the organization (a more detailed analysis of the importance of mentors is in Chapter 5). The new senior manager was a gentleman named Owen Brown. He was tough, fair an excellent executive and someone who was easy to follow. He turned out to be a mentor who would help me throughout my career. That strategy helped me move to my next position, a second-line management slot, called district manager, with over sixty sales reps in the group. There, I gained valuable experience in managing through others, and learned some valuable lessons. When I was the district manager in San Francisco, we had the first district in the world with more female sales managers and sales reps than males, and it was a real breakthrough. They were highly motivated, aggressive, charming, and intelligent, which resulted in our district being the number two in the world during both years I managed in San Francisco. I learned early that having a diverse staff can produce results not otherwise attainable.

Managing through others also requires real leadership, as you do not have direct contact with the people in your organization, but instead have to rely on others. This requires setting direction, and establishing a style and tone of how the group is going to operate. It requires constant working through the managers and maintaining relationships at multiple levels. There are many cases where you can observe junior or first-line managers telling employees to refrain from talking to the "big boss," or if they do, to only tell positive news. I believe that if you show leadership, and have strong relationships, you can work through bad news as well as good. We worked hard at motivation using contests, prizes, recognition, promotions, and money as positive incentives to achieve the best results.

The real lesson was in how we achieved those results. We sold big, spent pretty big, developed very large accounts and had a great time. It was the most exciting and fun job of my entire career. ***The lesson to be learned is that to motivate people at any level you must have two important levers. First, you must pick very good people (most important), and then create an atmosphere for success.*** If you do that, you will most likely overachieve on your goals. As I progressed up the management ranks, the second goal of creating an atmosphere for success became more difficult, but it was always part of my management philosophy. Over the years, often having fun meant spending money, which can be difficult depending on the company, the time, and the management. But it can also mean having fun going to a baseball game, a barbecue, or setting up a competition between groups in the office. It is not so much what you do, or how much you spend, it is getting the people in your group working together, laughing and having fun. ***A motivated team will most often overachieve their goals in any industry and at any level.***

I make it sound easy, and clearly working for a hot company with industry leading products was instrumental. But along with the fun and excitement came some difficult moments. People will try to take advantage of you, to get ahead or to try to shortcut the rules. Even in good times, one must always be on the lookout for these kinds of individuals. When you find them, work hard to remove them from the organization. That doesn't necessarily mean firing the person, but you must be prepared to do so. ***My*** *philosophy always was that removing someone who is not performing is extremely important to those who are staying.* They are watching, they know what is happening and how, when and if you remove that person, you earn the respect of all of those who stay. That is what is most important. One difficult moment for me came when DEC was several months late delivering its hot new product, the VAX-11/780. We were a major vendor to the fast growing, new company called Apple, where we did the computing for all their manufacturing facilities. Apple could not bring on its new manufacturing plant without this new computer. After several delays, Steve Jobs, Apple's legendary CEO, ordered a ten-foot diameter black wreath delivered to Ken Olsen, the CEO of DEC, embarrassing Olsen, whose next call was to me to fix the problem. The fix was that we got the next VAX off the line and had it to Apple within two days. While the two industry leaders were never friends after that, there was a great deal of respect as we were able to respond, despite being a bit embarrassed.

Sometimes leadership is solving problems outside your area of responsibility during difficult circumstances. *Another key to leadership is to listen and then act upon what you hear.* It does not mean you have to answer every request positively, but if your people know you are listening to their wants, complaints, and desires, they will begin to follow. Some would say it is easier to motivate sales people because they are motivated by money, and that is true. However, I have managed some of the top technical talent (software developers, database experts and product managers) in the industry at different jobs, and they were motivated, worked hard, and would come back to work for me again, which is a result of listening and leadership.

I have been criticized several times throughout my career for being too well liked and not tough enough. One manager said when we parted ways, "Rich, I did not think you were tough enough when we started working together, but I realize you manage using positive motivation, and you can and will make the tough decisions, up to and including firing people." I just did it without yelling, getting emotional or being a jerk. In my opinion, you don't have to be best friends with those that work for you, but I feel like positive motivation gets great results.

CHAPTER 5

The Role of a Mentor in a Takeover or Management Change

Developing and maintaining mentors may be the single most important factor in your career.

Everyone needs help and guidance, and someone pushing for them. No matter your position in the organization, having someone above you acting as your champion will help you get ahead. Staying with one boss for a long time has some significant advantages, and **having a mentor who will help your career is perhaps one of the most important strategies you can employ**. It is rewarding in many ways. You will be promoted faster and higher than others. You will get larger raises than others. If your mentor leaves the company, many times they will invite you to join them. The landscape is crowded with companies and executives who bring their team with them. Management wants to make certain that the team they pick will be able to overachieve, and more important, will follow their lead. I mentioned earlier that my first mentor was Owen Brown who had promoted me in San Francisco. As mentors often do, Owen was instrumental in my next move to headquarters working for a good friend of his, RoseAnn Girodano, who would eventually become my next mentor.

The decade of the 80s was my most serene in terms of management changes. For most of the decade, I worked for the same boss, RoseAnn, who was the first female vice president of DEC. There were few management changes or takeover attempts. RoseAnn became my mentor, and she was great. She was interesting, aggressive, smart, people-oriented, and it was really exciting to work for her. In a male-dominated environment, she understood how to thrive. DEC was still experiencing astonishing growth, and that meant good opportunity for most of its employees who were aggressively climbing the ladder. Two strategies emerge for times of calm like this. First, it is a good time to develop a mentor because you have a longer period of time to work together, which enables you to do things that will help or make your boss succeed. Many times in a takeover, the CEO will later go back to members of his or her team where there had been success, because they helped the CEO attain that success. The second strategy in developing a mentor is maintaining loyalty. ***Loyalty is a key strategy, and it must be given as well as taken.***

Many aggressive professionals expect their boss to be loyal and promote or reward them. My take during this great time in my career was to be very loyal to my boss, protecting her, helping her, and ensuring that both she and her group were seen as go-getters within the company. We exceeded our numbers, and were creative in our approach to our customers and sales teams. This resulted in ten years of professional growth, extensive international experience and travel, and increased responsibility. For me, it was the first time in my career where I was out of direct sales or the sales channel. I undertook opportunities in operations, product marketing, product management, and general management. However, we found ourselves in continual skirmishes with other groups, as organizations fought for recognition, resources, and favor. ***The most important learning was to take care of your mentor, always provide excellent service to your constituents, and never forget that the numbers always rule.***

An interesting story occurred toward the end of this period. RoseAnn was viewed as a threat by a more senior executive, who had an *attack dog* as his pet subordinate. This attack dog, very intelligent and also female, was well respected by the senior staff, and would set out to remove any rival seen to be a threat by her boss. As is often the case in these skirmishes, it is not enough to win. Someone has to lose, and in this case it was RoseAnn. After a period of constant negative visibility from the attack dog, during a senior management offsite meeting, RoseAnn was targeted and fell out of favor. And as usual in these times of difficulty, all of a sudden this person appears to have a disease and no one wants to be near them.

Here, loyalty kicked in, and I was able to console and work with RoseAnn through this difficult period. She was able to retreat, maintain her position, and eventually return to prominence. During this period, my loyalty never wavered. I told her that in meetings I could not always defend her, but she should feel confident that I would never join the crowd and talk negatively about her. I would remain loyal, help her whenever possible, tell her who and where the land minds lay, and what to do to avoid them. I remained loyal during a difficult period, perhaps to my own peril. To this day, RoseAnn, now retired, remains a good friend and one of the best mentors I ever had. As a corollary, showing that there is mercy in this world, several years later, very carefully, several of us were able to help take down the attack dog and force her removal from the company. Sometimes, good does prevail over evil.

The real question is, "How do you pick a mentor?" This is one of those questions with no single answer, but is important when thinking about a company that could be involved in a takeover at some point. When I look to pick a mentor, I seek out individuals with certain qualities that will match my objectives.

First, are they smart? I like to work for people I can learn from, that make decisions, and have a good understanding of the market, our position, why we will win, and what we need to do to get there.

Second, I like my mentor to be a good leader and a good communicator. I want to make sure my mentor will listen to input and does not have to be the only smart person in the room.

Values are very important to me, and I want to make sure my mentor is honest and respects people. I had one president who had a good track-record, was very smart, but had two serious flaws. First, he always tried to intimidate people—from an initial interview to dealing with any important transaction, his method was to always attack first. Second, he was not totally honest. I always felt he was involved in channel stuffing, with orders from partners not always having the customers behind them. While I did not make my numbers every quarter, I refused to do anything that was not legal and ethical. Fortunately, he was fired within nine months of my arrival, and the company put up for sale. You might have noticed I used the term *president* for him and not *mentor*. While we got along, I would never consider him a mentor, and he would have never picked me as his top lieutenant.

When picking a mentor, you also want to make sure you get along with this person and can connect on multiple levels. ***You will spend a lot of time with your mentor, who can even be your boss.*** You may travel together, work long hours, and be together for much of the time, so you want to ensure, as much as possible, that you will get along and have fun.

How do you make your boss your mentor? The easy answer is to always do your best and make the boss look good, and soon you will become one of the go-to people. That does have merit. ***The idea is to exceed expectations and make the boss win.*** There are several caveats with this. First, you don't always select a winner to follow. There were several occasions where my boss either was not as good as I had originally thought, or no matter what I did, I was not able to break through. Second, often with this strategy you are putting all of your eggs in one basket. Your boss may not win the beauty contest. If they do win, you are a hero. If not, you have wasted a significant time and effort. Also, be careful of your coworkers as you strive to become the go-to person. Most people do not take kindly to the one always looking to be on top. Terms like *kiss-ass* or *brown-noser* soon get attached to this person. It is a difficult line to walk to be a part of the team, to lead the team, to be the boss' pet, without being so obvious to turn off your coworkers. ***My advice here is to work to be a leader, without always playing kiss-up to the boss.*** I have always been strong in my beliefs, pushed back strongly when I believed in something, but also tried to be a leader to help the team, not just the boss.

The real key to developing a mentor is to help that person win. In this case, if it is all about you, you will lose. This is ***one of my most valued principles. In every case, the key is making the person above you look***

good. My daughter was the director of Corporate Responsibility of a large insurance/financial services company. She had a project where the new CEO gained recognition and power because of her program, and as a result, she became one of his favorite employees. I would continuously tell her, "Remember, it is all about him." It's amazing to me how this very simple concept is either not known or not adhered to, but when followed, good things happen.

Now that you have selected the person you want to be your mentor, and have gotten into their good graces, how will you know if they truly are your mentor and will be able to maintain and recognize this mentorship? Developing a mentor takes time. It does not happen in one or two visits or interactions. It happens over a much longer period of time—a good guess is that it might take a year or longer. ***Developing a mentor also takes winning together.*** If a CEO sells a company or takes it public, most often he or she did it with the help of the team. They won together, they battled together, and they worked closely together, supporting one another, covering for the others on the team, and most importantly enjoying the fruits of their labor. So that when another opportunity comes around, that CEO remembers fondly the work of the previous team, especially those that he groomed. You can tell generally who are the ones on the team that the boss depends on, seeks advice from and spend the most time with. In a recent case where I knew the president was not going to be my mentor, I would see him spending hours talking with his new teammates, and very little time with any of the old team members . . . a sure sign of trouble. His old friends or colleagues were responsible for his previous success, and those are the people he looked to as he moved forward. ***During your time with the new boss, pay close attention to how he or she acts.*** If it is always the business at hand with no time for pleasantries, or if the boss is always in a hurry, this is not a good sign. Management always has time for the people they like most.

CHAPTER 6

My Fall from Grace

Continuously take stock of where your company is in terms of the market and where you stand with the people who count, and do not be afraid to move on. You can then be in charge of your own career, instead of watching it happen to you.

It was now the early 90s, and Digital was beginning to experience significant difficulties. UNIX was becoming a big threat to the traditional customer base with the promise of cheaper, open computing. But the biggest threat that Digital failed to see and respond to was the arrival of the personal computer. The executives at DEC could not understand that the same movement that inspired the shift from large monoliths to the mini-computers where Digital was king, was now happening to them, as PCs became more powerful and were able to put computing in the hands of the users, in every field from banking to medicine. This same phenomenon happened more recently with the smart phones taking business and marketshare from the laptop computer vendors.

During this period I worked for a senior vice president named Bob Glorioso. He was smart, creative, well-positioned with the CEO, and very aggressive. Our group was one of three development/business groups in the company responsible for the high-end or large computers. We introduced several computers that were industry stars, in particular the VAX 8600 series and VAXclusters, which enabled several computers to work together in a single environment. Remember, in the early nineties that was not a concept readily available in the industry. This concept is still in wide use today almost twenty-five years after we introduced it to the market. As a group, we followed our leader and aggressively positioned ourselves to takeover other areas as well, like redundant computing and transaction processing, offering an alternative to the traditional mainframe approach to solve these large and important computing problems.

My position during this time was product line manager, the business manager responsible for the profit and loss of the organization. It was a big responsibility, with revenue of over one billion dollars. It was an exciting time as we were the stars of the company. I managed a group of over one hundred people responsible for the marketing, product management, business management and operations of the high-end computing group. It was clearly the apex of my career at Digital, and soon would be the beginning of the end.

The CEO of DEC, Ken Olsen was a big, powerful man, well respected throughout the entire business community. He would assemble his entire executive staff each month for the monthly business review. For some reason, my group, the high-end group, was always first on the agenda. As soon as I would start my presentation, he would slam his fist on the table and scream, "That is not want I want to see." This was very intimidating and frightening, and it was character building to understand that he was not really yelling at me, but wanting to deliver a message to his team. This happened often over several years, and truly did help me to understand how to remain calm during periods of crises. I learned a lot during that time, as he was one of the legendary CEOs who built a company from scratch to a multi-billion dollar enterprise. He did it with leadership, wisdom, honesty, taking care of customers, always doing the right thing, and with a passion for product excellence. The side not often seen was that he was tough, demanding, hard-headed, sometimes wrong, and a difficult person with which to work. However, no one said that they weren't much better off for the experience of working in that environment, and you can count me as one of those people.

We bet the farm on a new VAX mainframe. We beat out several rival groups to lead the company in this important area of growth for Digital. These were not skirmishes but all-out war, with most decisions being made at the most senior management meetings in the company. As often is the case with war, you do things you are probably not proud of to win the battle and the war. At this point, careers are at stake, including my own. In the end we won, and had the biggest, most elaborate product announcement and launch in the history of the company. The market was ready and early sales were promising. However, the product was not what we thought. There were product delays, early stability problems, and the ability of the mid-range product lines to produce larger and more powerful computers, at only a fraction of the cost. Soon important decisions had to be made with huge ramifications. Factories were operating to produce these large computers that were not needed if the sales were not as expected, and soon it was decided to shut down this line. We moved from aggressively marketing this product to figuring out how to save these very important customers. The executive vice president was soon forced to leave the company and eight of the eleven managers on his staff were forced out as well. I was asked to stay to help control the damage. While I survived the firing squad, I was probably shot and did not realize it. I was too closely associated with the team, as one of its leaders. I was rewarded for staying through this difficult period, and was able to attend a prominent executive management program, but the damage was done.

I stayed with the company for two years after this fall from grace, hoping that my reputation would get me through and enable me to continue on the fast track. However, I was wrong! It was not a good strategic decision. I was seen as damaged goods, both by friends and colleagues with whom I had worked for many years. I have few regrets over the twenty-one years I spent at Digital. I was treated well, paid well, promoted many times, and given responsibility not often available to a person who started with the company as a sales trainee. However, one of the mistakes I made was not realizing that I had been shot, and that my career there was done. This is an important lesson—***know when to move on***. I lost two years, and watched the demise of a great company because I did not act more prudently and quickly.

Continuously take stock of where your company is in terms of the market and where you stand with the people who count, and do not be afraid to move on. You can then be in charge of your own career, instead of watching it happen to you. This is difficult because it is not something we're are used to doing. How many times are we looking for signs that are negative? If we are honest, most of us would say not very often. What are some of the signs you should watch for? The most obvious sign is if you are being sought out for your opinions on important matters. Are you being passed over? How much time do you spend with the new boss? Is he or she comfortable being with you? Are your conversations a good mix of transactional, strategic and non-work related? Are others suddenly getting more favors from management? Many of these clues are subtle, but they are there and you need to be looking for them. Another clue to look for is how your coworkers are being treated. If all your friends or close colleagues are not winning, it is safe to assume that you also are experiencing the same quiet fall from grace.

CHAPTER 7

Before the Takeover, New Management Teams Are Brought in for Survival

Nothing is more important during this period than to show them that you are on the team and will do whatever they want.

As Digital began its demise, a series of management teams were brought in to stop the losses and turn the company around. First, an Anderson Consulting team came on board to show the company how to grow and win the services market. As is often the norm, a very senior executive joined and brought many of his colleagues with him. Soon enough, Digital was in the consulting services business. I was not in the know as to the cost of this venture, but there were many who would claim success, as Digital had a large business centered on providing consulting services to its customers. However, it is well known that is it difficult to transition a hardware company into a services or software company. Companies like Dell, IBM, HP, and many of the mini-computer companies have tried with varying degrees of success to make that difficult transition. In the not too distant past, HP split the company into a product company and a services company, with good success. In time, most of these large companies had to buy their way into the consulting business by acquiring large consulting companies. Both HP and IBM are now leaders in this space, both achieved through acquisitions—HP by acquiring EDS and IBM by acquiring PwC Consulting. While Digital became a force in the consulting business, consulting was never integrated well into the mainstream of the company. Though not a takeover, it was a management change that was at best difficult. Strategically, the services group within the company became one of its most valued assets, so that while the management change was difficult, and never totally integrated within the company, by almost any measure, it was a success.

Two other significant management changes also took place during this period. First, an IBM team was brought in to reverse the downward path in terms of sales and revenue. A very senior IBM executive and his team were asked to bolster the sales side of DEC, always considered a weakness. At this time, Digital was the number two computer company in terms of revenue, and had many large and very loyal customers. It would have been difficult to make changes that would have a short-term impact, and from my perspective, this management team did not make changes to reverse DEC's downward spiral. While IBM was clearly the industry leader with strengths in sales and marketing, little changed other than new management throughout the ranks of the 5,000 person sales organization. There were two reasons this did not work. First, the time period was too short to change such a large organization so steeped in thirty years of culture and doing business a certain way. Second, the sales cultures of IBM and DEC were totally different. IBM was a top down, centralized company with excellent execution. DEC was a distributed, consensus-driven culture where everyone had a say. As the new IBM managers were brought in, they really never won the hearts and minds of the sales force.

After about two years without significant results, a second sales management team was brought it, this time from HP. Again, there were a lot of changes in the management of the sales organization, but little that resulted in turning around sales. This was met with the same response as the previous change. HP was culturally much closer to DEC, so there was less resistance to the new management, but now the company was struggling and people were bailing out all over, including sales. Neither of these teams was able to make much of a difference in terms of the numbers; it was too little, too late. The company was very big and it was difficult to make meaningful change. It is like trying to turn an aircraft carrier in a small bay. It could not be done quickly, and Digital did not have time.

There is an important concept in a management change. When these teams come in to do a turn-around, *the existing managers who have been there for any length of time have a big target on their chest*. The thinking is that they are the problem, and if only they had done a better job, the company would not be in trouble. Having lived through several of these, it is important to show that you have knowledge and that *you can help the new management team implement the changes they want to make.* They were brought in to make changes, and if they think you will not or cannot make the change, you are of no use to them and will soon be gone. *The rule is, if they want to try a new program, you must enthusiastically support the effort, even if you had just previously tried to implement it and it did not work. Nothing is more important during this period than to show them that you are on the team and will do whatever they want.* When you try to tell them that their strategy has holes or will not work, you are quickly labeled as the problem. I have watched this happen time and again, and it is almost an imperative. On the other hand, they need help to implement their new program, and they need managers and executives that the people will trust and follow. If they view you as someone who can help them, you will have great value.

Now having spent over twenty years with the same company, it was time to move on. Someone asked me, "What was the point or decision that finally made you decide it was time to leave?" I was working for a woman who we had hired while on the West Coast. She was a hard charger who had progressed up the ranks rapidly. While she said she supported me, she was continually undercutting me with my staff. We worked for one of the new IBM senior managers who, in a strategy review meeting, could not get past what the title of the program would be. I decided in that meeting it was time to leave. If my senior managers could not be strategic and just get marred in the details, there was no way we could ever work well together. I had few regrets from my time at Digital, *but the one lesson I should have heeded was to leave when I was on top and not after the fall.*

CHAPTER 8

My First Small Company and a Near Takeover

My first lesson in orchestrating a takeover did not end well, resulting in hurt feelings and the first time I was fired. Maintaining good relationships when you leave is all-important.

Having made the decision to leave, it was time to turn my attention to the next move. First, I had to come to grips with the hard fact that being with the same company for over twenty years was not considered by most employers to be a good thing. Remember, I had always valued loyalty, but now I was being told that I could not do well in a small company, and that being with one company and doing well was due, in large measure, to the company. I decided after a short period that I would join a small well-run services firm called Migration Software that was owned and run by two of my mentors at Dec, Owen Brown and Murray Cook. I was brought on as vice president of Eastern Operations to grow a business in the eastern half of the U.S. It certainly was a difficult transition, to move from a position of having many people on my team and significant responsibility to managing only two people and understanding that if the carpet needed to be cleaned, it was my job to get out the vacuum cleaner and clean it. For the next several years with lots of help from my mentors, I was able to grow the business to several million dollars per year with a dozen engineers on my team and lead the entry into new markets. What did emerge at my position with a small company was the confidence that I could do well without the resources of a very large multi-national. ***I was***

able to manage some world-class technical developers, learning once again that managing using the proper techniques is the same with non-sales types as it is with sales people. Mostly, everyone wants to know that you have their best interest at heart and their back when things get tough.

In the end, compensation was probably the single biggest factor in the eventual breakup of our relationship. I always wanted to be making more compensation, and every quarter it seemed I came up short. I complained loud enough and often enough that the owners finally decided I should seek my fortune elsewhere. It was the first time in my career that I had been let go, and it certainly made me reflect on what I did and what I wanted going forward.

A short story about a situation that occurred shortly before our breakup that most likely contributed to my eventual demise. One of my key employees had gone over to a well-funded startup and wanted me to join her. Over the course of several months as she better understood the goals of her new company and her own position, she and I put together a buy-out of my entire group. In my mind, it was a win-win for everyone. Our current company would receive an infusion of cash, the acquiring company would get a dozen engineers to help them grow their services business, and I would be on the ground floor of a well-funded start-up with an opportunity to make a lot of money. Well, the CEO of my company did not see it that way. He saw it as being disloyal, and refused to consider the offer. In the end, it was too bad that we could not have made it work as we would have all been better off. But the mistake I made was putting the entire deal together without his involvement, leading to his distrust and eventual parting of the ways. The result was that I was fired for the first time in my life and it was hard on my ego. So while not a successful takeover, there were valuable lessons learned in this near-takeover. ***Loyalty, communication, trust, and strong feelings on both sides are all necessary ingredients for success.*** Without them, or when they go awry, so will the success.

Whenever you leave a job or position, it is key that you maintain good relationships. This was a difficult breakup as we had worked together for many years, and were friends in business and outside of business.

There were hard feelings on both sides, and for a while after leaving, the relationship suffered. Remember these were my mentors and friends. It took some period (several years) of cooling off, before we were able to become friends again. But it is an example of where you can and should try to rebuild or continue a relationship, even through a difficult breakup. It is like going through a divorce, where you know it is important to maintain a good relationship, but very difficult to put into practice.

I have been in management for over thirty years, from a first line manager to a senior vice president managing many people. I pride myself on my management and leadership skills. I have had many cases where employees came back to work for me after having left multiple times. I have had to fire a good number of people, layoff people and watch friends leave. It is always difficult. If I done correctly, they will see that it is not usually the manager's fault they are leaving. However, most of the time when people leave, it is difficult. Feelings are hurt, people don't usually want to see or tell the truth, and the boss is generally viewed as the bad guy. I always try to tell those leaving, ***"How you leave a job or a company is extremely important." It is a lasting impression and you never know when you will see the boss again.*** It may be at another company, he or she may be looking to you as the new manager, or often the boss is asked to be a reference from someone they know. Even with the new laws regarding what can and cannot be said by previous employers, the message is almost always conveyed. The perception of how you left is now the perception of how you are remembered. It is essential to maintain a good relationship with those who you are now leaving.

It was now a time period when I had my highest expenses with two kids in college, and I found myself trying again to figure out what I wanted. Opportunities did not exactly abound, and with every job that I wanted, I seemed to be competing with my ex-colleagues at DEC, which was difficult as many of my old enemies were now in a position to influence. All of my past wins now seemed to be getting in the way of a job I desired. After several months of searching and not finding anything that was interesting, I decided to go into business for myself doing both consulting and recruiting. I actually did well during this period, but did not like working by myself out of my home. I felt isolated and did not see myself being in this business for the long term. I learned a lot about myself, what I wanted, and what I did not want. I decided that by working for myself, I would not able to put to use all of the training in management and business that I had worked so hard to obtain. It was time to take my talent and head back to the corporate world. And guess how the next opportunity came to be.

CHAPTER 9

The Importance of Networking During Periods of Change

The most important concept you should practice throughout your career is called personal networking, *and with the use of social media, it is critical and simple to stay connected.*

Personal networking is the art of keeping in touch with your peers and mentors as you move to other jobs throughout your career. As you read this, I'm sure you're nodding your head and saying, "Of course." Now let me ask you, how many people are you still in contact with two jobs ago? My guess is most likely none. Then you might cheat and say two or three individuals. Do you know where they are working, where they are living, and how happy they are in their current job? *The first rule of searching for a new job is to get out your file of the people you know and contact them.* That is easy and everyone does it, but it is usually more difficult than you think it should be. It today's world, people change jobs, change locations and have cell phones with no directory assistance. So the very first step—getting your list together—becomes a difficult task. Certainly social media sites like LinkedIn, Facebook and Twitter make it easier to keep in contact with people as time goes by. However, even with those tools, most of the time we don't contact our friends or business acquaintances. *The key is that you need to stay in direct contact with people who can or have made a difference in your career.* This list is not as long as it should be or needs to be. A short email or Christmas card reminds people about you and gives them a small glimpse of what you are doing or where you are working.

Recently, I went to visit one of my favorite mentors. She has been retired for a number of years, and she said to me, "I get a great many calls of people looking for a new job, and while I can't help them as much as I used to, I certainly try, especially if I know of anything appropriate for their background. I don't mind the calls and it reminds me of the time spent together. But I get very few calls from old business contacts just to talk and let me know what is going on. I really enjoy those calls and visits the most."

Personnel networking should start with your first job and with the people who have the most influence on your way of thinking. I remained in contact with my first mentor throughout his career, and remained personal friends until he passed away, and even now I remain in contact with his wife. Most of my jobs have been as a result of someone I had previously known. It can happen in ways you would not expect. One of my favorite people, Errol Weiss worked with me as the delivery vice president of a services company. We worked together, traveled together, and watched out for each other for five or six years. When that company was acquired, we went our separate ways—he to a very large financial institution, and me to another security company. Six or seven years later, he was looking for a new system for his bank, and knew I was no longer so excited about my current job. During a presentation that went poorly despite his earlier briefings, he called the CEO of the company to complain about how poorly the sales staff had done, when they should have been the leader of the procurement. The CEO rushed in for a meeting to try and save the deal, and my friend said no to this opportunity. When the CEO asked my friend if he knew of a vice president of sales who understood this business, my friend said I will give you the name of the guy you should hire. Three weeks later, I had a new position.

I want to say a word about expectations from your network. First of all, as mentioned earlier, most people are not very good at staying in contact, so your expectation should not be that you will be pen pals. People are busy. They are usually well-meaning and well-intended, but almost never get around to reaching out or responding. So you should not expect much in the way of constant communication. If you are looking for a job, your expectation should be that you will get in touch with them and they will be happy to hear from you, and ask that you send a resume along. You will be excited and will rush to get them the resume. Then nothing happens! When they receive the resume, they will read it, and if they know of a position, will send it to HR or the hiring manager with a short note of recommendation. More than likely however, they will not know of anything and will not know what to do with the resume. They will put it on the pile, and most likely never see it again. When you call to follow up, this time it is more difficult to get in touch with them, and when you do, their answer will be they sent it on to HR, but did not know of any positions. It is not that they don't want to help, they just don't know how. This is not to say you should not reach out to everyone you know, because you absolutely should. Finding a job is a numbers game, meaning the more people who know you are looking, the better your chances are of landing a good opportunity. Having someone on the inside who can give you a reference is all important, and most likely will put you In front of others.

Now that I have impressed upon you the importance of networking, I want to give you a few tips *on how to make it work for you. I do believe social networks are the best way to stay in touch.* On Facebook, you can see friends who you have not seen since high school. In one quick visit, you can see where they work and more about them than is probably wise. But for your purposes it is great. You can reach out and let them know and all of their friends know that you are looking for your next opportunity. LinkedIn is one of the best for personal networking. You see all of your contacts, your acquaintances, and their contacts. Again, you can reach many people very quickly.

I work hard at remaining in contact with many people, but I'm not great at it either. I travel a great deal and often will look for an acquaintance in the city where I am traveling. I will have dinner or coffee with them and they seem to enjoy hearing about what I have been doing and who I have seen that worked with us. It is an easy way to maintain contact. *The last way of stay in touch is with email.* Most of the time, people's email addresses are relatively easy to find. Everyone reads their email, and it is addressed only to them. It is easy to forward the email to one or more people, so that your chances of getting your resume to an appropriate person increase.

Finally, ***the idea of personal networking is to keep in contact with people who can have a positive influence on you moving forward***. If they were important in the past, there is a good chance they could be in the future. My daughter recently changed jobs, and she had a good relationship with the CEO of her old company, who was many layers higher but worked closely with her and said repeatedly he was going to make her the *vice president of fun*. Upon her resignation, I encouraged her to send a note to him, and he responded that she should keep in touch. If she does, he will remain a possible mentor going forward, but if she does not make the effort to stay in contact, nothing will come of that, and it will be a missed opportunity.

CHAPTER 10

How to Select a Potential Takeover Company

There are numerous characteristics to consider at when trying to land at a company that's poised for an acquisition.

I am often asked, "How do I select a company that is a good candidate for a takeover?" If I knew the answer to this one, I would be wealthy. The truth is that there is no one answer. Every small company wants to go public or get purchased. It is like the American dream.

There are a number of characteristics that you should look for if you're interested in a company poised for an acquisition.

- Look at the market of the company. Is it a market where acquisitions are commonplace? Clearly, the technology sector is one example of a market with acquisitions happening at a rapid pace. Service companies, biotech and financial services companies are other such examples.
- Consider if there is a hot product or technology of the company under consideration. If said company has a product or a product ahead of their competition, that is usually a good sign, especially if that product or service offers clear differentiation over the market.
- Look at the reputation and experience of the management team. Obviously, if they have been through a successful transaction before, they are known and likely to be successful a second time.

- Research the management style of the company. Small start-ups are very demanding of your personal time (the twelve-hour day), and how the team works or doesn't is very important.

- Another important factor in these companies is the funding. Where are they with their funding sources? Where are they getting their funding from? How many rounds of financing have they incurred? By understanding their financing, you can potentially tell if the investors are anxious to get out or interested in the growth of the company, even if it means more investment. You can have the best product and management, but if you are not adequately funded, you will never have the resources to successfully bring the product to market.

- How many stock options are available and how many can you expect? In order to make this venture worthwhile, even if it should end in a buy-out, you must have enough options to make a difference.

- The final area to look at closely is a difficult one, and that is of timing. Many companies have most of the criteria listed above, but still struggle. In many cases, they might be too far ahead of the market. The product may be difficult to sell because there are few competitors and the market is too small or immature. In many cases, the venture capital investors behind the company are growing impatient and want to see their return or move on. This one is difficult to determine but can be very important.

I have had several people who worked for me that were chasing that dream of the life-changing buyout. In one case, Max, who worked for me on two occasions, left a good job with a good salary a couple of times, to go work for smaller companies where he could get significant stock options. How did it work out for him? Max left to go with a start-up in the security industry called WholeSecurity, which was eventually bought by Symantec. While he had a number of shares, and made some money, it was less than $50,000, and represented at least three years of hard work with below market earnings during that time. As soon as he went to Symantec, he left because he was offered a job selling all their products to the education market, of which he had no experience. The second time, he went as a sales rep to a startup in the financial services industry called Trusteer, which was purchased within three years by IBM for a huge multiple. This time he hit a jackpot. While it was not life-changing, it was a bit hit and enabled him to work because he wanted to and not because he had to. What was his secret? He would tell you he was wiser this time around and selected the company because of the product, the experience of the founders, the market demand, and that he had enough shares to be meaningful. All of which is true. But he forgot to mention timing and luck. You see it takes all of these attributes and more to align, and when they do, bingo, you are in luck and are in line for a big payday. ***There does not seem to be one attribute that is more important that the others.*** Maybe having the right product at the right time, not too far ahead of the market, or not too late may top the list. But having a management team that knows how to take the company through the various cycles, and a board of directors with enough money and patience to sell just at the correct time, is equally important.

One of the factors mentioned above is the number of shares of stock you are able to negotiate. In one of the companies that I was part of, I was the second largest shareholder behind the investors, with over 100,000 shares of stock. When we sold, I was certain that was my home run. However, the sale was done in two parts, an initial payout, which mostly benefited the investors, and a second payout dependent upon an earn-out that was equally divided between both companies. We made our share of the earn-out, but the parent company did not even come close. This resulted in no second payout to the shareholders. This was a bit frustrating, but there was little anyone could do. Even the investors were not happy. While I did fine on the first payout, it was not the life-changing payday that I had hoped.

CHAPTER 11

My First Takeover

When things are not going your way, buy time to enable you to put a strategy in place.

It had to be—a new opportunity, another mentor. A good friend and business colleague Harvey Weiss had just taken over as president of a turn-around security company owned by a large defense contractor named SAIC. The company, called Global Integrity, was losing over a million dollars each month and had gone through several management teams in the previous two years. The president contacted me and asked me to run his sales department. My reaction was that I did not know much about the security marketplace. His response was that he could teach me security, but he needed someone who could turn around a sales force. The only wrinkle was that I could not report to him, but had to report to the chief operating officer, a gentleman named Dan Woolley. Dan would have never selected a person who did not know the security market, but we got on fine and Dan became one of my biggest supporters and mentors. ***Here is a tip: you need to make a believer of your boss even if someone else is your mentor.*** Within six months of my new position, my mentor resigned and the COO, my new mentor became the President. Because of my loyalty to him during that first period, I became senior vice president of Sales and Marketing, and he became my most loyal supporter. Had I ignored or went around him to my mentor, there would have been no trust, which is the key to making any situation work. During that period, I could still talk to and tell my mentor what was going on, but never did I try to play one against the other or try to upstage or set up the COO, but instead gave him my complete loyalty, and it served me well.

This position was fun and very exciting. This firm had the best talent in the security-consulting field. They were well-positioned to be great, but had gone through a series of senior management teams who were unable to get the formula right. The result was losses that the parent company was unwilling to accept. We needed to move fast to turn this around before the parent would shut it down. Coming in from the outside, I quickly determined which of the existing team I wanted to keep, which of the technical product managers I could turn into sales people, and who and where I needed to recruit from the outside. *I have always been a believer in hiring senior people and incentivizing them to over-achieve.* Many companies talk about this philosophy, but few actually put it into practice. We did, and lo and behold, it worked. We began to increase sales significantly, win repeat business, and grow the business both nationally and across the globe. Soon we became recognized as the premier security-consulting firm, serving the largest and most sophisticated companies across many markets. Within a year, we were growing, moving toward profitability, and you guessed it, on the market to be sold.

This company represented several firsts for me. I had no experience in being brought into a company with the goal of turning it around. I did not have the experience to know the moves required to be made, like where to cut spending, how to change a sales team and product management team that had been at odds for several years, how to create an environment to quickly gain new Fortune 500 customers, or how to grow internationally and make it cost effective and profitable. I was the one brought in from the outside who had to make quick decisions that would affect both my group and how the company would fare in the marketplace. I had a personal task of creating a team made up of skilled, motivated, team-players that had experience with the security buyers.

The most difficult part of the job was the commute. You see, we lived outside of Boston and the job was in Virginia, outside of Washington D.C. Today, it is pretty common to see people working away from their home, but this was in the late 1990s, and the deal I made with the CEO was that I did not have to move, but I had to be in the office every week, because everything flowed through the senior vice president of Sales. As a result, I commuted from Boston to Washington D.C. every week for over four years. Several members of the management team were in similar positions, and we spent a great deal of time together. This ability to spend time as a team was very important, as we lived together, worked long hours together, and grew together. Many of the executives on that team now run the security organizations of the largest financial institutions in the country. We were able to accomplish most of the goals we set out for ourselves, and were profitable, growing and well positioned in the market.

My wife, Judy, deserves the credit for making this arrangement work. She maintained our home near Boston for four years while I traveled every week. She always said, "nothing bad ever happens while you are at home". It is very difficult to run a family when one party is only there part time. She did a great job which enabled me to accomplish my business goals.

The other first was that I had not been involved in an actual takeover and had no idea what to expect. And in early 2000, I went through my first takeover, this time by a consulting firm called Predictive Systems, headquartered in New York City.

My first thought about this takeover was that the whole ordeal took far too long. The result was a loss of focus and momentum. ***Everyone began to worry much more about who their new boss was going to be, and what their new position would be, and where they would be working, and, in some cases, would they still have a job.*** Predictive Systems was a fast-growing dot com company that had gone public shortly before buying us and was singularly focused on growth. The CEO and his management team understood well how to grow a consulting company, especially in the dot com era. They worked hard to make the transition into their company smooth, with committees, management meetings to plan the future, and a genuine desire to incorporate all of the people being acquired. A number of people on our team, including myself, were kept as a separate division to lead the efforts into managed security (the outsourced monitoring of security devices for large corporations). How could it be any better? I was able to keep my senior vice president title, take part in a start-up venture in a company that valued growth in a hot market for the industry, and had enough stock in the new company to be life changing.

So how did it turn out? Well, in early 2001, the dot com bubble burst. It was one of the recessions that people read about in the history books. All of the excesses of previous decades were now being exposed and eliminated. Consulting companies that had seen incredible growth, now were having to work under a new model called cost cutting and survival. Our CEO, who earlier had been trumpeted as brilliant, was replaced by a partner of one of the *big four* consulting companies. The new CEO was not any better prepared to lead in this new environment than the previous CEO, and we all watched our stock fortunes fall. To make matters worse, he was the first CEO in my experience who did not like me at all. I believe it was because before he had come, I had negotiated a deal that made me the most highly paid individual in the company, with a contract for a year's severance upon any termination. Mr. Know-It-All broke the contract, invited me to sue, and soon I left with some definite hard feelings and six months' pay. As for Mr. Know-It-All, he took the company with a stock price of $120 to less than $2 per share before he was struck with the same fate as me. I must admit, I got some satisfaction out of that one. When I look for the lessons learned during this period, it is difficult to say that I did anything wrong, or that I would have changed the way I acted. I had an internal competitor who was an incumbent and well liked, although in my opinion, not particularly good. I negotiated hard, maybe too hard, to be in a position of strength. The newly appointed CEO did not like sales, did not like me, and no matter what I did, the outcome was pre-determined.

One thing that stands out was the actions of some of the management team during the takeover, especially when they were in positions of power in the acquiring company. At Global Integrity (the acquired company from Virginia), we had a strong management team, and every member except the president and CFO were asked to join the new management team in the acquiring company. However, it soon became evident that the members of our strong team were looking out for themselves. Several of us felt abandoned by others on our original team. The takeaway from that experience is that ***during a takeover, expect team members to watch out for themselves as they try to win favor by the new team. No matter how strong the prior bond, assume everyone is out for themselves.***

The new CEO came to me and said that he wanted to sell the managed services division and get out of that business. However, he wanted to retain the revenue, which presented an interesting dilemma. After a bit of discussion with some interested parties, we were able to put together a deal where we would shut down our Operations Center, and let go of all of the people. We would transfer the cost and operations to our partner, and the revenue would continue to flow through us, subsequently moving seventy-five percent of the costs to our partner and retaining the other twenty-five percent for our efforts and maintaining the customer relationship, at least in the short term. While not a good long-term solution, it satisfied all parties. My reward for this strategy, shortly after the deal closed, was that I was fired, for the second time in my life. One strategy that can be employed during difficult times is to buy time. When I received the news of my termination, I was told that I had to make a decision by the end of the day as to what I was going to do. I was a bit in shock, but by the end of the day, said I would accept their offer, but wanted to speak directly with the CEO, which I knew would take weeks. After some wrangling, we were able to settle on six months' severance. It took over three months before I was let go, so I ended up only three months short of my original contract. ***When things are not going your way, buy time to enable you to put a strategy in place.***

We did not get to reap the rewards we all had worked so hard to achieve, and that was certainly disappointing. However, for me personally, I had a new career, an established track record, and a wealth of experience in turning around a business, and now my first experience of being acquired. I could set out on my next venture with the confidence that was sure to position me head-and-shoulders above my competitors. In other words, I could become a free agent.

The major takeaways of this first acquisition were several. This was my first opportunity to be in the driver's seat of the new management team. By moving quickly, establishing a very strong team, solving some long-standing internal political rivalries, and creating a reputation as an industry leader, we were able to create an environment where everyone— our owners, our employees, and our customers—believed in what we were doing. When our firm was eventually sold to Predictive Systems, they did many things right in incorporating our firm into theirs. Few predicted the fall of the dot coms, which hit the consulting community especially hard. The new CEO was brought in to stem the losses and change the culture. He was never able to do it, and the company floundered for several years before being sold to a competitor for pennies on the dollar. While he wasn't very good, and did little to stem the tide, I am not certain anyone could have changed things enough to stay viable. What I do know, was that for me personally, it was one of the best experiences of my working career.

CHAPTER 12

A New Company and a Family Move

There are a number of key contributors who make a difference in the company. In an acquisition, you want to be on that list.

Searching for a job is truly one of life's most challenging experiences. Even coming off a great experience, having a good reputation, and knowing many people in senior positions, it still sucks. We had been in the Boston area for over twenty-one years, a bit longer than the two years we had initially intended. The entire family liked it and it had been very rewarding. However, five years after Digital had been sold to Compaq and the number of workers had gone from over 140,000 to less than 40,000, New England had still not recovered from the economic shock. While some of my old colleagues at Digital were now in key senior management positions, most had strong views on their past friends. Either they felt like DEC management hadn't been strong and were biased against these people, or they remembered you as you were ten years earlier. While they had grown and matured, you were not thought of in those senior roles. All of this told me that maybe I should broaden my horizons and look for work outside the Boston area. Our children were now out of the house and the family was receptive to moving. Soon my previous mentor and president Dan Woolley called with an opportunity of another turn-around security company in the Washington D.C. area.

This company, Silent Runner was owned by a large government contractor, this time Raytheon. They wanted me to join, but with the caveat that we had to relocate. I negotiated that I would move after nine months of commuting, as I wanted to make sure the job would work out before making such an imposition on my family. ***It is important to test drive an opportunity before making major life changes.*** Oftentimes in these turnaround or new positions, while done with great intentions, reality may turn out not as good as was originally intended for either party, often resulting in the parties splitting. When you have moved your family and are now in a place where you don't have a personal network, you are at a considerable disadvantage. In my case, both parties lived up to the agreement, and within the year, our family had moved to Northern Virginia. The boxes were not yet fully unpacked, when we were called to an important meeting and met the new management team installed by corporate with instructions to package the company up and sell it. The old CEO was out and the new president and vice president of Sales was introduced (remember, I was the vice president of U.S. Sales). That day was not one I will easily forget.

What was I going to do? ***The key is not to panic or overreact.*** This is much easier said than done. My approach has always been to be a leader who managed using content, not just style. I had personal knowledge of every customer and every prospect being worked on by the entire sales force. The new management team knew nothing about our products, our strategies, or our markets. I had the knowledge and quickly became one of the valued, go-to individuals. I had to do a lot of jobs that I was certain would not result in new sales, and I had to play to a new management team that I did not necessarily believe in, but ***my strategy here was to buy time.*** I had to make myself valuable and buy time for them to sell the company, which was actively being shopped on the market. It took almost six months before a buyer was found, and we were sold to a company with a long history of acquisitions and a horrible reputation: Computer Associates (CA), the company where good products go to die.

Now began a real learning experience on acquisitions—first being takeover by CA and then working with their management team as they did additional takeovers. When the sale was announced, the management team that had been brought in was asked to leave, and did so within a week, without even so much as a party or get together to thank everyone for their hard work. While we had known for some time that the company was on the block, this acquisition happened at lightning speed, which was the style of CA in almost all of their acquisitions.

Once again, Human Resources was in charge. The business units who were behind the acquisition met with some of our management team, but Human Resources was running the process. My group was broken apart and went to work for various sales managers in their respective locations. We were told that this was the CA way, and not given a choice. The down side of this is that as a sales vice president, I not only lost my vice president title, but lost all control of most of my people. We kept a small team to drive the business across the corporation. We essentially became an overlay sales team, brought in with product and market knowledge to assist the sales teams around the globe. All of this happened within two weeks. Everyone was offered a position, but we had no time or knowledge of what was going to happen. We signed up, and signed all of the non-compete paperwork, or were told we would not work there . . . and if that was the choice, there was no severance. So, I decided to become the director of a product line and gave up my coveted vice president title.

CA was in a period of real change. Their legendary and autocratic founder retired and several of the senior managers all left at the same time. A new management team was brought in from IBM to change the culture of the company, long considered by customers, and employees alike, as a very difficult company to work for or with which to do business. The new CEO brought in a huge cadre of vice presidents and set about to change the culture of the company. In general, he succeeded. While remaining aggressive and hard-charging, supporting the customer became the norm. Another one of the shifts they wanted to make was to change the culture of how they acquired a new company, starting with us; for the most part, it worked. Most of our managers ended up in other management positions and were still associated with our product line. We were able to retain most of the key contributors of the old company. My mentor and the one responsible for my being with Silent Runner was Dan Woolley. He was in a position similar to mine and decided to go to CA, so while in a different group, we were able to work together for another four years.

There are a number of key contributors who make a difference in the company, in every discipline. You certainly want to be on the list of key contributors. Figuring out quickly who those key individuals are, and putting in place retention plan to keep as many of those as possible, will help determine the success of the acquisition. In addition, it will help other key personnel who want to stay as the leaders and who have bought into the new regime. As the product line manager with all the responsibility for the profit and loss of the product, but with few direct resources, keeping those people with knowledge and drive was everything. Our acquisition was touted as a success and served as a roadmap of how all future acquisitions should be done. As a result, I was brought in as part of the management team as new companies were acquired to explain how good it would be, the pitfalls of the new company, and how much CA had changed. Each acquisition that I helped with was different, and often it was largely dependent upon the line organization responsible for the success of the acquisition. ***Key for the acquiring company is that the more involved the line organization is in the early days of the acquisition, the higher chance of success for retaining the top people, and having the products or services be integrated into the business of the new company.*** If you have the opportunity, or if the acquiring company has not provided much access from the business unit targeted for your company, take it upon yourself to meet with and understand that business. It will serve you well as teams are formed.

From the perspective of the employees, CA had changed and for the better, as they were now much more friendly and caring, and listened to the needs and desires of the acquiring personnel. From the business perspective, after watching a number of these happen and being on the inside, I believe the acquisitions that worked best were those where CA left the acquired company to operate as a separate company or division. This was not the norm, as they usually used the acquisition as a model and integrated the groups within their existing organizations. However, when there was an acquisition where the company had a big reputation or market share, they were left as a stand-alone subsidiary snd integrated over a longer period of time.

Because there are so many factors that play into what makes an acquisition successful, it is difficult to generalize that this organizational style will always be the most optimum or produce the best result. However, when you get a motivated workforce and management team with some degree of autonomy, change is minimized, and they are less subject to processes and the rules of the acquiring company. The downside is that they are not generally as integrated into the new company and strategies as if they reported directly to the new management. An example of a change to this style is to look at the recent acquisitions of IBM—these companies are left to maintain their previous identity while being part of the IBM family. Although, even they use both organizational methods as they acquire new companies.

Another key factor for acquisition success is to keep the knowledgeable people from the old company tied to the success of that new business, while figuring out how to operate within the framework of the existing company. They can then move or disburse the personnel after a period of time. The important factor here is that the key people are not asked to make quick decisions and report to individuals they do not know. When they still feel valued, they are much more apt to stay and be a productive member of the new team. When done in this manner, I have observed very little talk of legacy company versus new company, but instead much more of a spirit of cooperation and willingness to share.

I spent four years at CA after the acquisition, and it was a rewarding and fun time. Each year, our product line got a bit smaller but they liked our products and the WOW factor in demonstrating that they had leading-edge technology. Our small team had several world-class members in Jason Mical who could make the product do amazing things and Yiannis Vassiliades who was a fabulous product manager, which was key in such a distributed organization. We were also able to keep our small development team which allowed us to stay in front. However, the product never really fit in to their security strategy. They liked our overlay style, and my small team would travel worldwide and make sales in new markets. We were a distributed organization of less than ten people, but we were able to make sales they had not counted on around the globe. So while not a financial success, we were well loved throughout the entire company. Our boss was located out of the state, and we only saw him two or three times a year . . . mostly when I would travel to him and take him to lunch. While we had a great time, we also knew this gravy train could not last, and we began the process of spinning out and selling our little product line. After several false starts, and more time than I wanted, we sold the product and customer base to a company where there was a much better alignment of the product with their corporate strategy. Just about that time, I was offered a position in another turn-around of a security company, so it was time to move on. Many years have passed since my little product line was sold to Access Data, and I am happy to report it was a strategic part of their new company, and almost all of the key players remained and were involved with that product. It wasn't until recently that that they decided to exit that business and shut down the product line. However, it lasted and flourished for over twelve years. As for me, the experience meant one management change, one acquisition, and finally selling off the product line and watching it grow and survive in a new company—so it was clearly a success.

One final thought about CA's style of management. They liked us, and we were well compensated, but after losing our vice president titles, the one thing they never figured out was how to get the best out of us. We were pretty senior and could have helped them in many areas outside our area of responsibility, but that was never what they wanted. They never wanted us to do more, or let us feel like we were important. Once we figured that out, we were able to deal with it, but it was a bit disheartening and demotivating. All in all, the time with CA was time well spent. We were like a small business in a very large corporation. Our vice president was in a far-away location and never very visible. I was able to consult with a number of their newer acquisitions, working with management to set expectations on life at CA. In the end, I worked on selling our group to a company whose business was more closely aligned to our product. While I did not go with the sale, it worked out very well for all parties, as the entire team spent the better part of the next twelve years with that company.

During that time, I watched and was a part of a half dozen acquisitions and was able to help figure out what worked and what could have been done better. As I think about those acquisitions, several factors jump out at me.

- The first is the size of the company being acquired—in general, the larger the organization, the more difficult the integration.
- Second is the success of the company or product being acquired is dependent on the retention of key employees and management. Very successful companies have managers who would do a better job than the new managers who typically do not know the product or market space. These managers tend to stay only for their retention bonuses or until they find another position.
- *Finally, the two most valuable positions in any acquiring company are the product developers and the sales engineering group.* In many cases, the acquiring company will do a good job of courting the developers (especially the key developers) but then do a terrible job retaining the technical sales engineers, who know the product, the market and how to present why the customers should buy. In almost every case that organization is never highly valued.

CHAPTER 13

Another Turn-Around
and the First Sale

Acquired by a Government Contractor with pleanty of expenience in takeovers meant high expectaations from all parties.

When I left Computer Associates, I went to work for another security company who was in trouble, Cyveillance. They had seen success, but struggled to become profitable and had been around longer than their venture-capital backers wanted. They had gone through several management changes, and while they had an industry-leading solution in the market for monitoring the internet, they had lost their way in sales. I was replacing a first-time vice president of Sales, and she was a total flop in every aspect. Her team did not respect her, and the CEO was frustrated with her total lack of understanding of the marketplace, what the company did well, and the lack of leadership in directing a very junior sales force. ***One of my key strategies is to never follow a Lombardi or Gates, but instead follow a manager who has lost their way.***

This was an ideal situation for me. I understood how to sell to the largest corporations and had a strong Rolodex of key leaders at the world's biggest companies. I was able to bring back members from my previous sales teams, quickly sell to the industry leaders, and begin the turn-around. The CEO, Panos Anastassiadis, was fabulous—a big Greek who was passionate, knowledgeable, fun, and the team was excited to work for him. Within a couple of years, we were able to move to break even, which had been difficult as a software-as-a-service (SaaS) company. More important, we were able to establish ourselves as the industry leader in a space soon to be called *cyber intelligence.* The threat landscape had changed from protecting the perimeter of a company's network to threats now coming from the internet, from outside the country, from nation states like Russia and China, and from the new phenomenon of computers on mobile phones and social media.

We were preparing to be sold and had many of the ingredients working in our favor. We were a hot company in an emerging market, with a technical solution that many companies wanted. And a customer base that was the envy of every small company. The year was 2008, and the country was in the middle of one of the worst recessions in its history. In hindsight, we should have not been in such a hurry to sell. But the investors were pressing us, and the CEO received an offer that was too good to pass up. There was only one problem—the offer was from another defense contractor, this time QinetiQ North America.

There are many difficulties with a takeover of a commercial company by a large defense contractor. First, there is the market and how they operate. They sell to the federal government and are good at knowing their customer and how to deal with them. We were a company whose market was ninety-five percent commercial. That makes for an incompatible mix. The goal was to be able to take our services into the government. They were a services company whose main metric was time-sold, and we were a SaaS (Software as a Service) company worried about recurring revenue. They made decisions by committee, and most decisions took a long time. Our CEO made decisions quickly with the advice of only one or two people. Defense contractors buy small commercial companies for their innovation, but in many cases drown the very innovation they are trying to achieve and run off most the key contributors. I have been involved in three different companies where we were owned by well-known, well-run defense contractors, and in many cases all of the parameters described above hold true. There is always a great desire to make it work, and certainly it can and does work, but it is never as easy as it should be.

However, let's move back to the question at hand. The acquisition was pretty textbook and did not take as long as ones I had been through previously. QinetiQ had acquired seventeen companies in the two years before our acquisition. They had the process down to a science. The deal was a good one, with an earn-out that would net many of the key players a good sum. We were excited because we thought they had resources we desperately needed to stay ahead of the market. If we could capture market share in the federal space, we would continue to be the undisputed leader in this new and exciting market called *cybersecurity*.

Soon after the acquisition was finalized, Human Resources took over and did a good job. This time, most of the key employees were taken care of and retained. The entire management team was kept on, and we were left as a wholly owned subsidiary. This had the promise to be done correctly. We could continue to run and grow our business, have new resources, and they could help selling into the government market. It was a perfect takeover from the start . . . or so we thought.

CHAPTER 14

After the Takeover

The most successful takeovers are typically those that are left as their own units—this buys you time.

In the summer of 2011, almost two years after we were taken over by the defense contractor, the CEO, Panos was forced to leave. ***As is often the case when a company wants to get rid of an executive, they used a familiar formula—buy him out and reduce his authority to the point where he can make no decisions.*** This combination almost always works. The president or CEO of the company being acquired is used to making all the decisions. He or she is the boss. After the takeover, the boss now has to report to someone in the new company. Many times the larger company makes decisions by committee, or the committee has to approve. It starts with small HR-related issues under the guise, "That is not the way we do business at this company." However, over time almost all decisions—important ones like budgets, raises and product decisions—must be approved by *corporate*. Occasionally, the acquiring company will let the new company continue to run as a separate entity. While I have not done a formal study on this issue, ***my instincts and experience tell me the most successful takeovers are those left to run as a separate group, with a significant percentage of the management team and employees kept as a part of the new team. If you are involved in a takeover, this especially is important to you because it buys you time to see how the new company is run, and how you will fare. You always want time to be on your side.***

In our case, for the first year and a half, we were left as an independent subsidiary. The entire management team remained with the company, and we continued to grow. The relationship with the parent company was never that great, in large part because the parent had the business model of a services company and refused to put more needed capital into the acquired company. They were a large *beltway bandit* taking over a small, entrepreneurial company who sold to the commercial market. Almost nothing was compatible. The reason for the purchase was to have them utilize our technology to capture government business, but after two years, very little had been done to go after or sell into that market. The Greek did not like or respect his managers because they knew nothing about our business, and tried to force a round peg into a square hole. The best example of this was that after twelve years as a SaaS business, one of the first changes they wanted was to make was to have us use a *services* business model. This transition was not easy, as all of the customers, contracts, and revenue recognition were all based on the SaaS business model. The result of two years of this meddlesome-management style was that Panos's authority to make any decisions was now almost completely gone, and it was time for him to move on. Uh oh, things were about to change.

I had put together a strong team of the best sales people I had ever seen. Jim Swinney had been with me earlier as my International VP moved to Japan. He was brought back and sold 17 new name Fortune 500 accounts. Thomas Johnson, a graduate of Duke University and trained at IBM was the best enterprise sales rep ever. Don Sortor was a security consultant who was also with me at Global integrity and who has the best rolodex of senior level clients. Eric Baum also worked for me earlier and was great on the West Coast opening up a dozen large clients. And finally, Jim Martin was the VP of Sales Operations and my right-hand man. For many years, Jim made sure the team had what they needed to have the best customer base in the security intelligence market. Our customer base was excellent because we hired sales reps with experience, provided a team environment to help them succeed and paid them well.

And change they did! First, one of the corporate lieutenants was brought in to bring us under the mothership. He was a good guy, with no commercial experience, but who would follow orders, and his orders were to make the company profitable and grow the company by fifty percent. Most respectable business schools would tell you that you need to choose one or the other, growth or profitability, but that it is very difficult to do both at the same time. This period was one of cutting and consultants. We cut projects, we cut spending, and worked to try and keep our people. A high-priced consultant was brought in to look at sales, and get rid of me and any of the sales staff she felt were not capable. After three months, when she reported back that the company did not have a sales problem, she was quickly shown the door. When the year did not produce the results they wanted, a long and difficult search for a new president was concluded, and the new wunderkind was found.

CHAPTER 15

The New Requiem

After an acquisition, do things the new way—the boss's way.

A management change occurred with a lieutenant of the parent firm brought in to bring us under the corporate umbrella and make us profitable, while they looked for a new president. This was a time of great change, as most of the management team was replaced by the president's new team.

The new president was young, aggressive, knowledgeable, and had a background in our industry as a marketer. It does not get any better than that because he also had a background in government and a degree from a military academy. It was easy to see why he was hired. He had everything. Throughout the following year, I watched every theory in this book come to life. For starters, we had world-class talent, like the vice president of Delivery who had all the attributes a security firm would want—smart, talented, and a good leader, with intelligence experience. It did not take long for her and the new president to come to blows, resulting in her resignation. Her replacement was brought in and was a disciple of the boss. Before long, the Development vice president resigned, frustrated with the new style and directions. Not long afterward, the Channel vice president also had a contentious resignation.

It was clear, the old guard needed to be moved out, and their replacements were friends of the new team. There are a couple of signs to watch out for during this period. ***First, your opinions do not count. Your experience*** *and record do not count for much either. Do things the new way, the boss's way.* The second thing to *watch for is the president's relationship and dealings with the new members of the team.* Every small decision is hailed and broadcast to the troops. The new members will do anything they are asked, and will always agree with the boss.

Look out for a lack of your communication with the new team, at any level. My dealings with the boss were always transaction-oriented, in other words, something that had to be dealt with immediately. There was never time or interest in just talking about last night's game, my family or the latest water-cooler discussions. At the same time, the new members would spend lots of time in his office (next to mine) discussing everything but work. This was a sure sign of trouble ahead.

Another troublesome sign is to watch your power and authority slowly slip away. The sales force was tremendously loyal to me and we had done very well over the past five years. This bothered the new boss, and he thought I pampered the sales force. All pricing was taken away from Sales and given to the delivery teams, who had no idea of how to price and were given no training. He said this was done to make the delivery managers more accountable and to empower the sales people to make more decisions. The result of this decision was a slowdown of the process, frustration in the sales force, and a lot of internal negotiation to get to the desired result. Next, a new contracts manager was brought in to restore order and discipline in our contracting process. Finally, the commission plans were dramatically cut, with the goal of refocusing the sales force on to new business.

How did all these changes work out? The company had been growing at twenty-five percent per year for a number of years, was the envy of every small start-up, and we had a client base of the top firms throughout the country and abroad. We were nearing profitability in spite of the fact that several new products were discontinued as they neared release. The following year produced mixed results. We became profitable because we significantly reduced our expenses by removing almost thirty-five percent of the people. The parent company was pleased because we were profitable or near profitable each month. The sales force was downsized by a third, and commissions for the remaining sales reps were cut. Morale was not high, as raises and bonuses for the non-sales staff were significantly cut back or eliminated. The sales staff that had been so successful now could not sell new accounts and were phased out or forced to quit. What was clear is that there was one person who made the decisions, and like many in positions of power, some of his decisions turned out well and others failed miserably. While we made progress on becoming profitable, sales and revenue fell back. There were less sales people, with low morale, and a lack of trust of the new management team.

The president's goal was to grow the company to $100 million from $20 million, almost impossible to do organically in a SaaS business. He had a new plan, product or opportunity each month that would enable us to get to $100 million. Many resources were spent on chasing down these new opportunities, only to fail as they took us away from our core business. On the positive side, he made decisions on what he believed the customers wanted or would want in the future, and was very customer focused. With all this going on, and the eventual hand-writing on the wall, it was time for a new strategy for the old vice president of Sales, me. It was clear that I was not his chosen one, and now only a short time would transpire before he would want a change. I needed to figure out quickly what I wanted to do so that I was the one in control.

CHAPTER 16

Strategies for Moving On

It is always difficult to move on, to change, and to leave a job you like. These are the human factors that are almost always present during a takeover.

Many years earlier, when I ran the San Francisco sales district for Digital, I hired Bob McLuen, who was my first manager and who I described in Chapter 1 as the boss everyone followed. At the time, Bob was working at Olivetti as the branch manager in a dead-end job he did not like, but he needed the income. I convinced him to take a job as a senior sales rep working for me with one of our largest accounts. It was a marriage made in heaven. Bob was great, and the account produced beyond our expectations. We subsequently hired his wife and daughters in various jobs, all of whom were successful. Bob was able to finish out his career, enjoy his job, and retire to his house on the lake. I always said that was the way I wanted to finish my career. Now was the time to put that plan into place.

I approached the president and let him know that if he wanted to make a change and bring in a new vice president of Sales, I would work with him to make that happen, and I would like to be a senior sales person. He had already made changes to three other vice presidents, and I knew I was on his list. I knew that by proposing this alternative, I was making it easy for him. I had the experience, the contacts, the knowledge of our products, the knowledge of how to sell this set of services, and the respect of others in the firm. The seed was planted, and we had several bad quarters in a row, and he quickly jumped to make a change. After several weeks of negotiating my new job, title and compensation, we shook hands, and my new/old career began again.

I would not expect everyone to follow this path. Giving up significant salary, status, title, and respect is not easy or to be taken lightly. My point here is to recognize exactly where you fit with the new management, and put a plan or plans in place. When you read some of the signs I discussed earlier and they are not coming up in your favor, you should begin your planning.

The most likely strategy is to begin to look for a new company. Searching for a new position is never fun. The recruiters will call during this period as they watch the news for takeovers and know people are in a time and position to change. ***The best time to look for a job is when you have a job.*** I can't tell you how many people I have watched get frustrated and leave a company where they have a good position and are making good money. If you leave before securing another job, the first thing that happens is you lose your leverage in negotiations. The new company knows you don't have a job and they can be much tougher in their negotiations. **If you leave before having a position locked up, do not expect to make more money.**

The second problem with leaving earlier than you should is that you tend to take the first position that you are offered. You do not have an income coming in, and you are not sure when and if you will get another offer. This results in taking a position where you might not have as good an opportunity going forward.

Here is one final bit of advice when you are in the position of looking for another company. ***It is imperative that you maintain a very positive attitude in your current position during this time.*** This is very difficult, because you no longer like it there or like the new management, but it is all important. If you are negative or disruptive during this period, it will be cut short, because they know that you will not be around and will want to move on with someone else before you are ready. This is particularly true during large meetings. An example of this happened with our vice president of Channel Sales. He was so negative in company meetings and would question every decision in open forums, which resulted in his dismissal and a lawsuit with both parties losing in the end.

Another strategy you can employ when putting your plan together is to transfer to a different division or department. Many times a takeover occurs when a large company takes over a small one. This is a time for opportunity. As the new team is getting to know you, you can take that time to look around inside of the acquiring company. Management is more tolerant during this period, especially if it is in the new company. Just be careful, as it may also be construed as a sign that you do not want to be in the group they have slotted you. I believe however, it is worth at least taking a look. Remember, the management team is new and has not yet figured out who their go-to team is yet.

I want to bring up one other option for your plan. *If you believe you can win over the new management team and become one of their go-to people, this may be the best of all plans.* It can mean a promotion, a raise in compensation, and for certain, an opportunity to become a valued member of a team that should give you longevity. This will take away many of your initial fears. The question is how to win them over, and how to read the signs. My experience says *the best way to win over the new team is to provide exceptional value*, so that without you, it is difficult for them to implement the changes they want to make. They have to quickly recognize your value and reach out to you as you are looking to help them. Remember one of my first tenets: *it is all about them. If they see you as a key player to help them win, you will be in.* And then the fun begins.

How quickly will this happen? There is a school of thought that many senior managers follow, and it involves a ninety-day plan. They want to be in a position after ninety days to have a plan to move forward. While not followed uniformly or always formally, it is a good rule of thumb. The first quarter, no one expects a change in results; however, they do expect the new team to have a plan that will move them in the direction they want to follow. *Ninety days is pretty quick, so you want to figure out what your value is, how it helps the new team, and how you will*

ensure they recognize your value. This is a time to be especially honest with yourself as you assess your value and how it will help them. It does not pay to be over-zealous or over-inflated. They will quickly see through the junk, and it will kill your chances. However, ***I would say if ever there is a good time to build trust, now is the time.*** Be interested, be supportive, ask for help, and most of all have a good attitude. Do not whine, tear down your colleagues, or overly question their evolving plans. The more you spend time with them, and genuinely buy into what they want to do and show them how you can help them, the more likely you will be on the team.

As a recap, three options for you to consider as you make your new plan include:

- Begin to look outside while you have a good position and the world knows and expects people to be looking so the search community will reach out.
- Look within the acquiring firm for other opportunities
- Take a position within your organization that allows you to be on the new management team as one of their people.

My point here is that you should view this time as an opportunity to improve your position and stature. Sometimes it sounds negative and it can be, but it is also the time to get ahead. These times of change will enable you to get on board with the new management team or find another position where you can blossom going forward. ***While change is always difficult, it is the time where the most significant jumps in your career will occur.*** Take advantage of the opportunity.

CHAPTER 17

My Option: The Path Least Traveled

Check your ego and keep your eye on the prize.

As I mentioned earlier, I chose a forth option, to take a demotion and a cut in salary to become a senior sales person. It is worth a bit of discussion as to why I would choose to take this option. First, I had seen it work before, and in fact had been a part of making it work, so I knew it could be successful. Second, because it was a sales position, while I took a large cut in salary, I knew I could make it up with commissions. My age also was a factor. Being over sixty-five, finding a new position as vice president of Sales would not be easy, as most companies want a younger, more energetic sales leader. I also knew that in sales, when you change companies, you have to expect a significant drop in your earnings for the first year as you learn the new company and the new products, develop a new sales pitch, build a sales pipeline and then actually make a sale. So when I weighed the options, the best option was to stay where I was, as I knew the products, the customers, and how to sell them. I also had some negotiating leverage (although, not a lot) as to what accounts I would cover. By taking some of the largest clients where I knew the decision makers, my plan was to make up for the loss in salary, make myself very valuable to the company, and work for several more years.

As many years have passed, and I am happy to say that my strategy worked well. I proved my value and was given the largest and most critical accounts. I became one of the go-to guys. They understood that if I left, it would have had a dramatic effect on their sales and revenue. Remember my key motto: make yourself very valuable. I found that I could work as long as I wanted, so for me, it was the best strategy.

When choosing the plan to take a demotion and stay with the firm, the first thing you have to do is **check your ego**. Now that is easy to say and very difficult to do! I had been a manager or vice president for most of my career—thirty-eight years. And I have to say, I was pretty good at it with all of my companies and positions. I liked being the boss, making decisions, taking calculated risks, helping develop my groups and working with senior-level people. Most of my people liked, respected, and produced for me. Now with one handshake that was gone. I realized that to make it work, I could no longer be the boss or try to be the boss. While I had lots of experience and knowledge, the difficulty was that for the most part, no one cared or asked for my opinions. A difficult aspect of this strategy was to refrain from responding when the president made a disparaging remark or a decision with which I did not agree. For the most part, those remarks were not directed at me, but were made to give me a shot like, "The sales force was terrible and could not sell," when he knew I hired all of them.

The key is to **keep your eye on the prize**. My goal throughout this process was to work for several more years, to continue to make money and save for retirement, instead of retiring early and drawing down my retirement fund. Our sales people made a lot of money, so selling here meant having a leg up on the sales process. I knew the product, the accounts, and where the most likely new opportunities would exist. The only question was, could I make this work for several years. Soon after I stepped down, they hired a new vice president of Sales Doug Dangremond, and it took a while for him to realize that my goal was to help him succeed. While I did not agree with many of the early decisions he made, I kept them to myself and worked hard to support him and his new policies. After several months of learning to accept my new position and the reality of stepping down being harder than I expected, I liked my new job and was good at it. I transitioned smoothly and made my quota, and grew the key accounts, so the new management team understood that these accounts liked and responded to the experience and knowledge that comes with age.

I did have my days where I would get frustrated as some inexperienced person made a dumb decision that affected my ability to do my job. For a while, I felt disrespected, but I think that is part of the game as well, and it certainly got better with time. Most of the people in the company were great and made me feel important. It wasn't that they didn't like me; it's just the way it is. Years later when I looked back, I realized that most of those feelings were in my own head, and **what I needed to do was follow my own advice and keep my eye on the prize, understand what I wanted, and let the rest roll off.**

CHAPTER 18

The Master Plan

The key to personal success in any takeover is to develop a plan. This makes you a free agent with the confidence to have several options. You approach the situation with a new-found energy and a great attitude. You are now in a position to determine your own future.

I begin this chapter with the idea of bringing together many of the concepts and theories I have discussed throughout the book. I want to review them because whether you are the team being brought in, or the team on the receiving end, you can learn many of the techniques and observations that will be used as you undergo a takeover.

First, if you are lucky, they will let you run as an independent group or company. However, more than likely, they will begin the process of integration. **Remember, integration usually means doing it their way and making sure you know who is in charge.** Soon, the old boss will be forced out or will want to leave. That is when they bring in their person, the wunderkind. He or she will be looking to make changes, and to bring in his or her own team. This is usually the most difficult and discouraging time, as old bosses and friends are forced out and the new people are the unknown. You have no relationship or history with this new team—they know it all, and you are an idiot.

Because takeovers are change and change is difficult, most people are afraid and become timid or unsure of themselves and their position. While this is natural, I want to give you another way to look at this situation. First, as pointed out earlier, ***take stock of your position, your reputation and your accomplishments.*** If the outcome of this self-evaluation is positive, think optimistically and boldly. ***You are about to build your Master Plan.*** This is very important because it puts you in a strong position to determine your own outcome.

You will in many ways start over, and should realize that most of the time, you will leave. It is not bad, you have not lost, but the trick is to do it on your terms. Be smart, plan, do not argue or fight the new directions. ***Decide on your own if you can make it, if you want to make it, and put your plan into place.*** When you are the driver, good things happen. You feel confident and confidence breeds success, all because you have a better understanding of how this process of the takeover goes down. Make it a time for a positive change and the opportunity it brings. It is certainly understandable that most people don't like change, and especially one as important as a change in their job or responsibilities. However, positive change can be a difference-maker for your career. It does not have to be a negative experience.

If you actually write down the plan it will be more comprehensive, you will know where you want to be, and the steps for getting there. Some considerations as you make your plan include:

- ***Be honest with yourself as to your value,*** both as a part of the team and to the new company. Most people tend to think that their job and how they do it is far more valuable that it really is. This does not help you. Be honest. If you do a good job, and have been considered a key performer in the past, make sure that function will still be considered valuable by the new team. ***This is a good time to get a second opinion of your value, preferably from someone higher in the chain, so that you might get a more honest opinion.*** How and where should that opinion come from? Two ideas of where to seek help. First, it is best if the person you ask is an executive or manager in the company who knows you and your work well. By asking that person, you force them to think about it so that when they are asked later by someone in the new company, they are better prepared. Ask many questions, always with the idea of assessing your value. Second, ask questions of your previous manager. Remember, the most important part of this exercise is to ascertain your value from the perspective of the new management team. Be honest with the answers and listen well.

- **Quickly assess whether you like the new direction as it is shaping up and the new management team.** In every job, in any company, your happiness and success depends on your manager. So the second step is to decide whether or not you want to be there working for this team or this manager.

- **Show the new team how you are helping them to achieve their new goals.** Earlier, we discussed that during the first ninety days you are selling hard and possibly using some of those political skills to show the new managers you are on the team, and if possible want to be one of the key leaders of the team. Be realistic in setting your goals for the new team. You are probably not going to jump multiple layers on the organizational chart. However, it does not hurt to try during this period to jump up one more slots on that ladder.

- **Throughout this entire period you are watching for the signs.** Are you making progress, do they see your value, is your value on their critical path, do they like you, do you like them, and what is making you think this? **Remember, every job is a two way street, and while you are being evaluated, you also are doing an evaluation.** You are like a free agent. If you follow these key steps, you will take the mystery and uncertainty out of this uncertain time.

The other thing to remember is that you do not have to be in sales to have these tips work for you. They work for development, for delivery and for operations just as well as for the sales and marketing departments. While many of the stories told throughout the book involved my experiences as an executive in Sales and Marketing, they only illustrate the point being made. Everyone wants to feel safe in their decisions.

My key takeaway is that you have to be in charge. Do not just let the change happen to you. There are occasions where that will happen. When it does happen, buy time, make a plan, and be diligent upon executing the plan. That way, you will certainly come out on top.

CHAPTER 19

The View from the Top

What drives an acquisition from the eyes of a CEO? In looking at the idea of a takeover and how it affects the people involved (the human factor), I wanted to get a view from someone who has experience from the top. I asked my friend Neil Ferris, who has been involved in many takeovers as a CEO and other positions, to work with me to understand the takeover from the point of view of the CEO or board of directors. As mentioned earlier, the CEO is acting in the best interest of the stockholders represented by the board of directors. Neil, now retired, is on several corporate boards and acts as a consultant for a venture-capital company on a number of start-ups. The following represents how he views a takeover and his action steps when he takes over a new company.

The best or most successful transaction is defined by a number of dimensions. As I've mentioned throughout, the first and most important dimension is if the investors get an appropriate return or their expected return. If they did, the transaction will be deemed a success. While there are other important factors, the market will judge the takeover from the perspective of investors. Another important dimension of success is how the new company does financially after the acquisition and if the acquiring company helps. In other words, was the new combined company better off for having made the deal? Were the acquiring products, people or technology instrumental in the company moving forward?

In most transactions or takeovers, the value of the transaction, or amount of money the investors are willing to pay, is driven by one of three reasons or interests. One is that the company buying wants your product or technology. Second, they may want your sales force or access to your customer base. Finally, they may want your development team. ***Remember that the members of the board are primarily interested in making money.***

Success can also be viewed from a second important perspective—did the key employees also win? Did they too make money from the transaction? This usually is accomplished by forward vesting their stock options in return for staying with the company for a certain period of time, usually twelve to twenty-four months. These key employees and management team members most often are the reason for the success of the acquired company and the reason the transaction happens. No responsible CEO feels good about a transaction where only the investors win. It would be very difficult for him or her to get people to join the next venture if these folks are left out of the winnings on this deal. In one of Neil's companies, greater than ninety percent of employees stayed with the company for several years, which was a sure sign of a good transaction. Another important factor of employees winning is if the people being acquired have ongoing roles in the new company. If the employees are able to have important jobs where they made a real contribution, they most likely will want to stay and contribute.

The acquiring management team must live with the company after the transaction. Therefore, the prevailing thought that the acquirers are not interested retaining as many people as possible could not be farther from reality. Yes, it is true that there may be jobs lost due to overlapping positions or efficiencies needed as a combined company. No company needs two human resources departments, finance teams, or accounts payable organizations. If you are in one of these support departments, your job is clearly at risk. Understand that the acquiring company has a duplicate organization in place, and their management team is known to the executives. As a result they will most likely have the upper hand in managing their department post transaction. However, in smaller companies that do not have large support organizations, the result is not a dramatic. Managers are generally quite accomplished and are able to get things done without large staffs so that they are well positioned if they wish to remain with the new company. In his book, *surviving the Merger*, Professor John Gomes states that many mergers are done with the goal of cost savings. His research finds that there is a drop in headcount of over thirty-five percent across all mergers. ***The takeaway here is that if you are in a support organization, and are involved in a takeover, you are at risk.*** You should quickly determine what the new organization is likely to look like, take a very realistic look at who is managing your corresponding organization and their status within the new company, and make a decision as to your desire to leave or fight hard to stay with the firm.

If you are on a customer-facing team, in many cases your value is very high. Whether it is customer support, sales support, delivery, or sales, most likely they need your expertise. That also is true for product development or engineering. They need your expertize to enhance the current product suite or to develop new products. In many cases, your team is likely to remain intact and command great value. Remember, they do not have the expertise to do your job or the job of your team. This is not always the case, as companies like MacAfee often will let the entire sales force go when they acquire the company, or they will put together an overlay sales force to assist their mainline sales force. As mentioned previously, Computer Associates is an example of a company who managed using this technique. Again, the takeaway here is to determine as quickly as possible the intent of the new management team, and see if this is what you want going forward. If not, begin to make your plans to exit quickly during this first three-month period. Although, be mindful there will most likely be a separation package, and it can be much better than just resigning.

Getting back to the earlier question, what is the driver for a takeover? This is important because it will guide the actions of both companies. Market conditions play a very important part in an acquisition and the value of the acquisition. There are several kinds of acquisitions from the acquiree (the company being acquired) perspective. First is the case where a company needs additional resources. A large company generally has money or other resources like people or marketing to help finance new product development or growth. Second, if the market is consolidating or in a period of dramatic change, and there is a need for the acquiring company to move forward with a new product, this would be a reason to do an acquisition and certainly play into how much they would pay to get what they wanted.

When does a CEO get involved with the staff of a company he or she is taking over? Most of the time when a deal is being discussed it only involves the CEO, the CFO, and one or two members of the board. All discussions are typically held off site and strictly confidential. A leak is one of the things that can query a potential deal. If you are the CEO or CFO, you realize that most likely you will not remain with the company past a transition period, usually less than a year. It is not until a deal is structured, agreed upon, and signed that the executive staff and members of the team are brought into the discussions.

CHAPTER 20

The CEO of the Acquiring Company Evaluates the New Company

After a CEO completes the acquisition and understands the financial aspect of the deal, there needs to be an evaluation the people just acquired. Remember this is a two way evaluation with you evulating them as well as the reverse.

What is the first thing a CEO does when assessing the new company? Usually he or she wants some kind of a non-financial analysis. The entire executive team will sit down and thoroughly brief the new CEO on the company. This includes everything—human capital, customers, employees, what is good, what is needed to make it better, their assessment of who they are today, what are the challenges, and what resources are available. This often is called the soft culture of the company, and involves the kind of people in the company and who makes the decisions. They also are evaluating if risk is acceptable. An entrepreneurial company getting purchased by a large company like a Fujitsu or Intel is a huge culture clash. The new CEO is trying to find out how the new company reacts, what decisions get made or don't get made. He or she wants to walk out of those meetings with a feeling of "I kind of get it now," along with the state of the union and the condition of the enterprise. This is not a financial discussion, but is very important as first impressions are often lasting. It will most likely be the first time the new CEO interacts with the management team and the key contributors, and he will walk away with a strong first impression. ***You want the CEO to think, "This is a person I want to move forward with on my new team."***

What are some of the characteristics the CEO will look for in evaluating the team? ***First and foremost, open, transparent leadership.*** Can they clearly articulate what the company is, where they are, what the priorities are, and where are the trouble spots? What are some possible strategies or solutions? The CEO also will look at their analytical capability and ability to articulate the state of the union, without great reservations.

Next, is this an honest person? Is he or she solid, ethical, trustworthy, do they think about team and greater good versus themselves? The CEO ***will look for and try to judge competency***—do they have the command of their area of expertise, whether it be Human Resources, Sales or Finance. Do they know what to do, and are they confident in their answers? ***Finally, is this person strategic and not just tactical?*** In other words, are they able to describe where the company needs to be in one year? The CEO will then look at the person's reputation among their peers and the management team. Is this person respected by their peers as well as those that work for them? Can they lift up those that work for them? Ultimately, the CEO is trying to ascertain if this is the person that could run the organization a year from now.

To review, the primary four attributes a CEO is looking for when evaluating the new team, include:

- Open, transparent leadership
- Honesty and trustworthiness
- Competency
- Strategic thinking

The bottom line is that if the CEO is not sure, ***the inclination is to take a pass or make a change, because it often takes as long as six months to see actual results, and he or she does not want to wait that long.***

The most important reason the company is successful is the people, and how they interact and react, which defines the culture of the company.

Teams must know how to collaborate and get the most out of the people. The management team must know what they are dealing with in moving the company forward. Engineering schedules, customers, competitors, key individuals, and the market are all factors that the CEO wants to know about during these first sessions. Finally, the CEO looks for confidence in their capabilities and if they collaborate with others in the organization. Do they have a shared vision and shared goals? While that sounds like a lot to take in in only a few meetings, it is the most important job a CEO has to do. If he or she is able to get in tune with key individuals at multiple levels, it will help form the new leadership team, and go a long ways in determining the success of the acquisition.

CHAPTER 21

The View from the CEO of the Acquired Company

As the new company begins integrating their acquisition, a number of dynamics are at play that can have an effect on the employees of the firm being acquired. What should these employees look for, and how can they use their current management team, especially the CEO, to their advantage?

The CEO of the company being acquired knows that he or she will most likely not be around very long. While there are exceptions to this rule, most of the time the CEO and CFO will be asked to stay only through the transition period to ensure a smooth transition. What are goals during this period, or put another way, what makes a smooth transition?

Most likely, the CEO is now working on his or her reputation. Their financial situation is known, and as long as he or she stays during the transition period, earnings are now predetermined. There is usually a bonus and/or a stock option tied to ensure the proper outcome as defined by the new company. Sometimes there is an earn-out to ensure the financial outcome expected during the transaction. Now however, the CEO is working for his or her reputation and wants to ensure the team is well adjusted. There is a perception that CEOs are only worried about themselves. However, by doing well by those who helped get him or her to this point, there is a ready supply of talent for the CEO's future endeavors.

However, the CEO is no longer the person in charge, and even if the acquired company is run as a separate company, there are new people to answer to, and a new level of trust and understanding needs to be developed.

For the employees and the management team of the acquired company, this becomes the best time the CEO can help. He or she has the greatest access to the new CEO and can be very influential in the selection of the employees asked to move forward in key positions. It is in old CEO's best interest to get the team well positioned.

How should we treat this lame duck CEO? *The key is to remain loyal and keep in touch, but to be viewed as moving toward the new management team.* This is usually not done very well. You may often hear the term legacy company versus new company. This is generally a sign that the transition is not going well. Cultures are not working. People are entrenched in their views and unwilling to change. A good example of this was when Digital was acquired by Compaq and the company cultures were completely different. The integration team did a terrible job of bringing together the employees of both companies. Several years after the acquisition, you could hear people talk about legacy DEC or legacy Compaq. People are either viewed as loyal to their old team or unwilling to move to the new team with gusto. Alternatively, they move very quickly and are not viewed well by the old team. I have seen that happen in almost in every case.

On memorable example involved a president who was not moving forward and was being overly protective on every decision with his original management team. Several of us were signaled out as moving too quickly to the new company and shifting loyalties. It is clearly a precarious position, and *my rule of thumb is to remain in contact with the old boss, but to shift your visible loyalties to the new company.* Always remember however, that last impressions are often lasting impressions, so it is important to maintain a balance. In general, if you had a good reputation and relationship with the outgoing boss, he or she will remember that in the future.

In some cases, the acquiring CEO will be asked to serve on the board of directors of the new company. While that sounds great and it can have some positive benefits, often it does not turn out so well. Neil had it work both ways, although looking back he would have preferred not to serve on the board. It restricts the movement of stock options, and in at least one case, he was never accepted by the other board members, and left both the board and the company within a year.

The CEO of both the outgoing company and the new company are clearly important as you make your plan to move forward. ***First impressions are key, so being prepared for your first meeting is all important.*** You most certainly want the new CEO to view you as a leader with a track record and reputation for getting things done, and with the leadership skills to help move the company forward. Confidence and presentation are very important. However, while first impressions are most valuable, the CEO will look for input from others as well, and here the outgoing CEO can be most helpful. These decisions are some of the most important he or she will make in determining how successful the takeover will be viewed in the future. ***Always remember, this too is a two-way street. You are evaluating the CEO as well, looking for clues to ensure this is the person you want to follow going forward.*** In many cases, depending upon the parties involved, you will not ever meet the CEO. Either you are not high enough on the corporate ladder, or the company is very large, like CA or IBM, and their CEO does not get involved in this level of detail. All of the advice also pertains to meeting the head of the unit responsible for the takeover.

CHAPTER 22

Selling the Company
Again a Second Time

Key to survival during a disruptive time is confidence, experience, perseverance, and patience.

Could it be happening again and with the same principals? It was clear that the marriage between Cyveillance and QinetiQ was not working at any level. There were not many options except to replace the entire management team and bring the company closer under the umbrella. However, this would take time and more money, both unacceptable to the parent. The other option was to sell the company. The thinking was that they could get out at the same price they paid and only worry about the operating losses. It could happen relatively quickly and they would get out whole, and be rid of this bad decision.

The Wunderkind moved on to a bigger and better opportunity. He was frustrated that our company did not fit in to the strategy of the government contractor, and he tired of never getting the investment he felt he needed to truly grow the company. Many of the old guard employees felt like this was his plan all along—get his ticket punched as a president, establish a couple of years of running the company and showing progress, and then move on. The aftermath was still to be determined, but the word was on the street was "Cyveillance is on the block again." Almost all of the signs began to play out. First, the parent company did not replace the president but put the vice president of Sales Doug Dangremond, now considered a mentor in as an interim president, with the assignment to keep the company moving forward and make it attractive for a future buyer. That is always a clear sign. The powers that be do not want to do a search for a new president, and more important, do not want to have to compensate the new president. By promoting, even on an interim basis, one of the current staff, they can instruct that person to prepare the company for acquisition, and give him or her a bonus if and when the company is sold.

The question now was not if, but when, and to whom. The former president left in April, much to the delight of the most of the employees. The parent company hired a company to sell us, and, of course, everything got remarkably quiet. These are the signs to watch for: the president, chief technical officer, and the CFO were suddenly gone for long meetings that lasted several hours to a day; expenses were being trimmed; and when people left, they were not being replaced. A recent reorganization along vertical lines had stalled the growth. This was an intelligence company, so it was relatively easy to watch the proceedings. Employees were spending a lot of time around the water cooler discussing alternatives and how it will affect everyone. This time, no employees had any stock, so the mood was excitement mixed with apprehension. The excitement was that it has to be better than working for QinetiQ, who was headquartered oversees and with whom the company was never a good fit. People were hopeful that with a new parent company, the company might get the investment it needed so badly. But clearly, many of those seminal questions also came into play. Will I have jobs, who will I work for, will I have to move or drive a long way? Should I begin to look for another job, how long will this take, and will we still exist as a company? Many of us spent many years building this company to have a great reputation, super employees (almost like a family), and one of the best customer bases in the industry. So while they were excited and hopeful that the new company would be better, the entire employee base was nervous.

As for me, the interim regime decided I was capable of managing a business and the people. As a result, I was named a managing director for the Financial Services marketplace which was our biggest and best market. Our results were above expectations. What is the reason I was able to survive these disruptions and still thrive? It was due to several key aspects. ***First is confidence.*** I knew the business well, and did well by our customers, who remained loyal and rewarded us with revenue growth. ***Second is experience.*** I knew what we needed to do to be successful, and put into place those actions where the whole team would succeed. These included making my entire team feel that they were contributing. We needed to make sure we had a customer-first mentality. Do the job and worry about getting paid for it later. My goal was to reward the people who over-preformed, and most important, to communicate with the entire team. And finally, I had ***perseverance and patience.*** This is probably the most difficult. The key was to figure out which battles I wanted to win, do a good job, and make sure they knew. This has served me well in the past in several companies, and I needed it to serve me one more time.

CHAPTER 23

My Final Takeover

Cyveillance was sold again after a difficult experience. The new firm LookingGlass Cyber Solutions had most of the qualities we would want; most important was that they felt that we could help them grow.

I want to spend a bit of time on the actual process that took place that produced the second takeover of Cyveillance. The parent company hired a firm to help sell Cyveillance. They first cast a fairly-wide net, with instructions to sell to the highest bidder. Our team made presentations to over sixteen interested parties, from competitors, to large consulting companies, to other threat-intelligence companies. The selection process ended up taking about eight months from when it started in earnest to when the transaction was completed.

There were two interesting takeaways from this period. The first was that using a sales intermediary seemed to add complexity to the process. Every meeting had to be in total secrecy at their office, and they worried about small details that did not seem to be important. The second was that the seller, QinetiQ, was difficult to work with and questioned every detail. Some of this is to be expected as companies go through their due diligence. However, sometimes it prevents important meetings and details from taking place. The acquirer, LookingGlass Cyber Solutions, said it was unlike their other acquisitions because there was not one integration meeting that took place before the acquisition was announced. The LookingGlass CEO Chris Coleman put together a long-term plan that included several key acquisitions and insuring that they integrated smoothly into his company. LookingGlass came in completely in the dark as to the most important aspect of acquiring a services company: its people. They had limited meetings with members of the management team, and did not feel like they had any understanding of either the people or the culture. That is important, because once the transaction was completed, within one day we were a part of the new company, with all the expectations that the combined company would work through the integration details that are usually started during the process of the sale. This was problematic because each company had a sales force, ours with a vertical organization and theirs with a regional focus. Also, our company has been around for over a dozen years and had good success in the commercial market, and their company was relatively new, with fewer relationships and a strong presence in the government.

LookingGlass was a product company with a business plan that represented a product company. They questioned how integrate this SaaS company into their product company and business model, and how to get the most out of the combined employee base and keep the key people. It would certainly be worked out, but now they were under the gun to have a strong starting quarter. In some departments, like Delivery, the employees did not know who they would work for, how they would be compensated, and if their skills would be needed or recognized. All of this could have easily been worked out with several integration meetings. *While integration meetings seem like they are only a process necessity, they are very important in helping to position members of a combined team, and alleviate many of the fears people have by sharing philosophy and direction.*

LookingGlass truly believed that the acquisition positioned their company to grow quickly and lead the industry in the crowded threat-intelligence marketplace. They did not have a true headquarters office, and decided to use the Cyveillance office, which meant none of our employees had to move, one of the other big concerns during a takeover. They also make it clear that no one would be let go, which of course was comforting. While several members of the executive management team did leave, it was their own decision. In other words, LookingGlass made good on their promise. Because Cyveillance had been around much longer, and was not very distributed, we had more advanced processes in place. Decisions were made to use those processes, which gave everyone a level of comfort. For the most part, there was little change in reporting structure, so that the staff knew their boss and how he or she worked. In the first chapter, I described why people get so nervous when a takeover is announced. Will I have a job, do I have to relocate, who my boss will be, and is there a good opportunity for me to advance? In the case of LookingGlass taking over Cyveillance, almost all of these questions had positive answers. Now several years later, when it is easier to look back and rate the takeover, I usually say that it was not perfect, and things could have been better. However, in this case, it was generally very good. Many of the key employees and management team remained in place, with jobs that were important to the executive team. Cyveillance services still are progressing and being integrated into the products of LookingGlass and most of the hard-earned customers are still very big supporters of the new company.

There were several areas where the integration could have gone more smoothly. First, like many acquisitions, everything seemed to take too much time, always fueling uncertainty. The timing of the transaction did not help, as it took place in mid-December, and then everyone seemed to go away for the holidays. During this critical period, nothing happened, and for the most part, all useful work came to a halt. The water cooler became the most popular place and speculation abounded. It was almost a month before discussions or decisions began to take place. One key negative factor was that the company name and reputation seemed to get lost, and the people of the acquired company felt like they lost their identity and culture. It was not terrible, and those feelings seemed to subside as time wore on and employees saw their products and services survive and thrive. However, clearly after sixteen years, theirs was a feeling of loss.

There were few retention bonuses or stock, and early on, the Cyveillance management team did not win any of the key positions in the new company but instead were forced down a level. Certainly, the new CEO wanted to have his management team stay in place as he trusted and knew how they would help the company grow. Also, while senior management talked openly about the importance of the newly acquired services, they never seemed to get the funding to continue to lead the market. My biggest criticism of the entire process was that they did not optimally make best use of the acquired talent, which would have helped the firm with their aggressive growth targets. There was a bit of arrogance that we are going to run it our way, even if the talent could have done it another way. This is much like the ball club whose new coach says we are going to run *my system*, even though he does not have the players who can make that system win. He would be better off altering his system a bit to fit the players that he has. However, as I stated earlier, overall LookingGlass did a good job of integrating Cyveillance into their company and using the talent to make the new company stronger and more valuable.

On the sales side, I personally had some struggles moving back from a senior manager position to a sales rep for the second time. It was not that I minded being a sales rep, but the new system was a regional sales model, meaning every sales person had a defined territory. For me, that meant giving up a number of my large accounts, and along with that, revenue and commissions. It also did not play to my strengths, which was selling and growing revenue base based on relationships. While I knew and liked my new vice president, I strongly disagreed with the way I was to be used and the transition plan to get there.

Here again is where many of my lessons come into play. I was unhappy enough to think hard about leaving and going elsewhere. Then a funny thing happened with my son who also was in the process of getting a new manager. My advice to him was that his new boss was not going to change his style, and that he could either adopt his approach to the new boss, or take his talents elsewhere. It hit me that perhaps I was thinking about that myself. I decided to quit fighting my boss, and adapt and support her plan. Wow, what a difference. As one of the leaders of the old team, whose opinion was generally respected and listened to, not only did it get better for me, but for others on the sales team as well. While she moved on within a short period of time, and never really became a supporter, we were able to coexist. She was replaced by a new chief revenue officer whose approach and style was much more conducive to the way I operated. I stayed on another year and a half, was successful in my numbers and account responsibility, and greatly enjoyed my time before finally retiring in June of 2018.

I discussed earlier how the most important success factor in a takeover is the return to the stockholders. While the return to the stockholders was not great, QinetiQ got out with what they put into buying Cyveillance and unloaded a big headache, so in the end they were satisfied. Everyone else won in this acquisition. LookingGlass was a stronger company after the acquisition, the Cyveillance employees felt good about the deal and their subsequent jobs. The customers were happy and continued to utilize LookingGlass, and the reputation of the company is stronger than ever in the past. Clearly, this time it worked.

CHAPTER 24

Decisions and Actions with Possible Negative Consequences

Reflecting back, there are several factors I wish I had known as I navigated by career, from learning how to sell up, to not getting in a hurry when looking for a new job, and that there is such a thing as to being too loyal.

Throughout my career, there were things that I think I could have done differently. I want to review several decisions or moves that I should have made, or perhaps if I would have made, could have had a different turn on my career. The first would be to *spend more time selling up*. I don't mean selling in the traditional sense of selling a product. What I mean is paying more attention to managers higher up the chain. I came from the old-school mentality that said your results should stand for themselves, and I thought if I did an excellent job at whatever my job was, that should be enough to get ahead. I've seen countless high achievers do an excellent job but get frustrated because they don't get ahead fast enough. This comes into focus even more in a takeover, as there is always a list of key contributors in the company being acquired. While each manager has input, your immediate executive is most important in determining who should be on the list. The list generally is reviewed by the members of the executive management team. If you have not spent any time with those managers, you can bet you will not be on the list. In my case, as the head of Sales, it was even more important. I did not spend enough time with the board of directors in most of my companies.

An example of this was in the last takeover, where Cyveillance was sold for a second time. By the time of the sale, I was running a quarter of the company, including sales and delivery. My group had done well, finishing second out of the four teams. The President, Dangremond liked me, so I felt like I was in a good position. However, the incoming management team viewed me as a sales person as opposed to an executive, and as a result, I was positioned in the new company as a territory sales rep, with no stock in the new company. From then on, I was treated as a sales rep in almost every aspect. I tried to explain that I could help in so many ways and that they were not using my experience, but the die was cast and my new vice president was not impressed when I would try and give her advice. As a result, I spent my last two years as a territory rep. This is not a complaint, as I stayed on my path to extend my career and make more money before retirement, so it worked. As I think back, this is one of the areas I could have perhaps done more to boost my career.

Another area that I touched on earlier, was when changing jobs, everyone—including me—tends to get into a hurry and is afraid that they will be out of work for too long, causing them to take the first job offered or settle for a much lower compensation package. Many times, people do not have a lot of money and need the routine paycheck. When in that position, they tend to lose their negotiating position and take the first offer. For me this occurred after I left the position of senior sales vice president for Global Integrity. I was coming off my best position where I had success in every way—position, results, compensation, and a successful sale of the company. As I mentioned several times, looking for a job is never fun. At that time, the market was in one of its lowest points ever, with the burst of the tech bubble. We were in a city that was hit particularly hard, and there were many executives on the street. I was able to get a good job, in a difficult environment, with a negotiated package that included a lucrative relocation package, but ultimately, I believe I was in a hurry.

As I have stated throughout, I have always valued loyalty. For the most part, it has served me well, with several mentors who rewarded me because of my results and loyalty. As a word of caution, you can almost be too loyal sometimes. That results in doing things that you probably wouldn't do under different circumstances or at a different time. I think about the time when I went after competitors in the company because of my loyalty to my boss. An interesting story resulted in this complete loyalty. I mentioned earlier about a new mainframe computer that we introduced at Digital and then removed from the market after just over a year, which ended up losing a lot of money. Shortly after we took the system off the market, the ax fell. Of the eleven direct reports reporting into senior vice presidents, only two of us were asked to stay with the company. I was asked to accept the job to head up the company's efforts to prevent the account base of very large and important accounts around the world from leaving completely and not buying all of DEC's other products. It was a very difficult job for which I was handsomely rewarded, including having the opportunity to go to an executive program at Stanford University. One day I received a call from one of the top three executives at DEC who asked me to come to his office. During the one-on-one session, he repeatedly asked my where my loyalty was, with my boss or the company. I said the company, but because I would not turn on my boss; that was the day I was really finished at DEC. I never recovered. Interestingly enough it was not just him either. His executive team, many of whom I counted as supporters, soon would not touch the spoiled goods. That was when I knew it was time to move on.

I've always considered my biggest strength to be managing and getting the most out of the people who worked for me. I was considered a players' manager, and that is probably a fair label. However, it has a downside. Many senior executives don't believe in that style of management. They believe that you over-pay your people and are too soft on them. They don't believe it is good to be so well liked by your employees. While I vehemently disagree with that, you should realize that the sentiment exists widely throughout the business community. While I am a sales person at heart, I have had developers, systems engineers, and security analysts work for me, and they are motivated by management that recognizes them when they do their job well. So while I would not change my style, *it is important to recognize that in a takeover situation, you will be evaluated by executives with varying styles, many of which may be different from yours.*

The final area that I want to mention that has caused some angst for me throughout my career is compensation. I have always negotiated my compensation package diligently knowing that once complete, you live with the results during your entire tenure at that company. However, in each of the times that I have been fired or let go, it was because I was one of the highest paid individuals in the company. Three of those times, it was after a takeover when new management took over. One of those times, I was recruited heavily by a new start up where I had good knowledge of the managed security space and this company put an extremely lucrative compensation package on the table. When I took it to the executive committee of my company, they decided to match it, and we were off and running. Several months later, walking down the streets of New York after a dinner with a coworker late at night, the recruiter called me and said the other company had looked at a number of other candidates and that they wanted me and upped the offer. I felt bad but told management and showed them the offer. To my surprise, they did not quite match the new offer, but came close. I felt like a major league player in a free agent situation. That sounds great, but there is a bit more to the story. I stayed with my company and was working diligently to show I was worthy of such a package. Shortly thereafter, the tech bubble of 2002 burst and our CEO was fired and a new CEO came on board. He was primarily interested in cutting costs and I was first on his target list—before long, I was unceremoniously released, despite having a contract. He never liked me because of my compensation package.

I don't apologize for being a tough negotiator on my compensation plan, but realize, like most good things, there can be a downside. My compensation got me on the target list again when I was at Cyveillance. As I mentioned in Chapter 14, the parent company specifically hired a consultant to prove why I should be fired. There was no question that one of the primary reasons was due to my compensation. Of course, it worked in my favor when I negotiated a deal with the new president to reduce my title and compensation package . . . and ended up making more as a sales person. I'm not sure anyone at the top ever knew.

I am certain there are other decisions I made during my career that had a direct effect on how things turned out. I have been told that I am a bit stubborn, so I am not sure how many of those decisions I would have changed, but in the end, I think I faired pretty well.

CHAPTER 25

Review of the Key Tips

In closing, here's a review of the key tips that I've given throughout the book. A takeover clearly is a time of change and change is always difficult. However, it also is a time to make your best moves and advancements. If you or your function is valuable, you will be well poised to come out in a better position than before. ***The key is to take charge and drive the conclusion, as opposed to letting it happen to you. You have much more power that you think. If you go into this process with a positive attitude and a willingness to adapt and drive the process, it can be the best time of your entire career.***

This period of transition also is a good time to evaluate. Do you like this new team? Can you contribute? It is a good time to look around, both inside and outside the company. The search community may be calling—be prepared to listen. During this period, be positive. Even if you disagree, sit on it or keep it to yourself. Project a positive image and show leadership skills. Everyone is watching and evaluating. ***People want leaders with a can-do attitude and a positive outlook.*** Remember, you are evaluating the new team just as they are evaluating you. It is a two-way street. You are like a free agent. Take control and you may land your best job ever. This is a good time to reach out to colleagues and mentors, but realize that for the most part, they will not be able to help you. Not because they don't want to, but because they either do not know of anything or don't know how to help. The most you can hope for is that they pass your resume on to someone else they know.

As you could see throughout the book, most of my jobs resulted from a call to a previous mentor. **I cannot stress enough the importance of developing, nourishing and most important, staying in contact with your mentors.** They know you well and can be of most help as you seek a new position.

It is the best time ever to make a plan. Write it down. It is not so important that you follow the plan to the letter, but use it as your guide to move forward in a positive direction. It is never fun to be in a position to look for a job, but if you have a plan, you can make positive steps forward, and not just see the rejection. The plan will enable you to have wins, not just to hope that your job will not be eliminated. It also will help eliminate surprises.

Understand that your most likely result will be that you will not stay with your existing company. This is not bad and not predetermined, but is the most likely outcome. Be realistic and be honest. Now is not the time to be overconfident. Your reputation precedes you. Far too many people over-value their worth to the company and that is not helpful here because an outsider, with little knowledge of you or your capabilities, will now be in a position to judge your value. In far too many cases, egos get in the way of sound judgment during this period, causing bad outcomes.

So move forward with confidence that many of the fears you had been thinking about getting acquired can be recognized and overcome. You can have more control, possibly getting ahead either in your firm or as you move on, but most important, know that you have a big say in the outcome.